HAMPTON~IN~ARDEN

A Village History

HAMPTON~IN~ARDEN

A Village History

Robin Watkin and Mike Bryant

BREWIN BOOKS

First published by
Brewin Books Ltd, 19 Enfield Ind. Estate,
Redditch, Worcestershire B97 6BY in 2006
www.brewinbooks.com

Reprinted March 2020

ISBN-10: 1-85858-286-5
ISBN-13: 978-1-85858-286-3

A Cataloguing in Publication Record
for this title is available from the British Library.

Typeset in Bembo
Printed in Great Britain by
4edge Ltd.

CONTENTS

Cover photograph. Solihull Road in the early twentieth century. The tithe barn is on the right just past the entrance to the Moat House. On the left are the Wheelwright's premises and in the centre West End Cottage.

ACKNOWLEDGEMENTS

Our grateful thanks go to a large number of village residents for their help in providing personal memories and other assorted ephemera. In particular we would like to thank Cecil Jordan for allowing us to reproduce the Spy cartoon of Sir Frederick Peel, and to Jane Coleman for allowing us to use her thesis, prepared during her college days, as a basis of the farming activities in the Parish.

Also to Maggie Williams, a past member of the history group, for her work on the public houses of Hampton-in-Arden, and to April Worthington and Pam Greenway for their memories of the Scouts and Guides.

We would also like to thank Ray and Pam Parker, and the late Maurice Roberts for providing and taking copies of photographs.

Numerous residents of the village, and ex-residents, have provided us with old photographs and they are too numerous to mention but we gratefully acknowledge their use in this book. We also acknowledge the use of photographs from the following. English Heritage (N.M.R.) R.A.F. photograph, Warwickshire County Record Office from DR(B) 63 box 9 and Birmingham Central Library

The authors also wish to thank the members of the local history group for their support in the publication of this book and in particular Sheila Denholm and Peter Kennedy in preparing it for publication.

We are grateful to the Parish Church for access to the Church and Village Chronicles and their various predecessors and also to the Women's Institute for use of their Scrapbooks.

Finally our grateful thanks to the Hampton Society for their generosity in providing the initial funding for the printing and publication of this book.

We acknowledge our use of the following publications.
Hampton-in-Arden. A Warwickshire Village by the Rev. J. C. Adams.
The Stonebridge Railway by Roger Waring.
Trading in Timber by Dennis Butler.
The Story of Hampton Cars by Trevor Picken.

INTRODUCTION

Growth and Development of the Village

THE EARLY YEARS

Hampton-in-Arden is located in the original Forest of Arden district of Warwickshire. When the Romans came to conquer in the first century this dense forest formed part of an almost continuous wooded belt which stretched across much of lowland Britain, forming a natural boundary between north and south. At first, the intention was to create a Roman province only in the 'civilised' southern part of the country, but within a century a few roads, like the Watling Street, had been built to allow Roman penetration into the north. They made no other uses of the dense Arden landscape, and it was not until the Anglo-Saxon invasion in the seventh century that the forest area was further explored. The Anglo-Saxons penetrated, mainly from the South West, along the Fosse Way and up river valleys, clearing areas in the forest for villages and fields.

Hampton-in-Arden owes its origin to the Saxons who founded a church and a hamlet on the summit of a hill above the River Blythe. Many variations have been given for the original name of the settlement - Hamtun, Heatun, Hear Tune - the high tun or high position above the river valley.

References made in the Domesday Book show the parish to be very much larger than it is today. It included Barston, Knowle, Hockley Heath, Nuthurst, Kinwalsey, Balsall and Chadwick End, and contained about 50,000 acres of woodland, but only 1,000 acres of fields, or clearings, which were widely scattered across the area.

In time the landscape would change considerably as more of the forest was cleared and re-claimed for farming, but during the Domesday Survey Hampton was a small clearing on top of the hill. The population in the original settlement around the church would have been small, most of the community being situated in outlying, isolated clearings or 'farms'. There were tracks or paths cut through the forested area for local use, not formally constructed, but trodden naturally by the continual use of pedestrians and vehicles. Hampton remained isolated, never being connected to any major route, and eventually these tracks would become the foundation of modern country lanes linking the surrounding villages.

A row of cottages called Sparrow Barracks at the junction of Fentham Road and Marsh Lane. The fenced area on the opposite side of Marsh Lane is the rear garden of The Nook, one of the original cottages in Crocketts Yard.

All this had a considerable effect upon the structure and population of Hampton-in-Arden, and no doubt other villages in the Arden area. Much of this timber would also have been used in the construction of new properties and farm buildings in the village and the outlying farms buildings as people prospered. Bricks for building were also produced locally at this time, more timber being used to fire the kilns.

Heavy red clay was abundant in Hampton and was excavated in a number of areas of the parish. These Marl Pits can still be seen in places, two between Hampton Lane Farm and Bickenhill Lane, wedge shaped depressions in the landscape, where the clay was hand cut from the vertical wall and dragged out up the sloping ramp. The brickyard was located in the north west corner of the parish close to Bickenhill Lane.

THE EFFECTS OF THE INDUSTRIAL AGE

In 1801, the census figures for Hampton-in-Arden show the population of the village of Hampton, together with Kinwalsey, was 406. The census of 1831 shows

A view looking down Marsh lane. It is difficult to place the exact position, but it could be around the area where Elm Tree Rise and Peel Close have now been built.

a more detailed picture, a total population of 593, possessing 120 houses occupied by 136 different families, of which fifty six per cent were chiefly employed in agriculture. This was a clear indication that a new structure was forming, and more people were seeking employment in a craft or manufacturing trade. By 1841, the village population was to increase to 781 and the Tithe Map produced in that year shows the spread of shops and small businesses across the village.

The year 1838 was an important date in the growth of the village; one single stroke of technological progress brought about considerable changes to the rural landscape and the farming structure. This was the completion of the London and Birmingham Railway passing across the northern edge of the village. In 1839, the Stonebridge Railway was built, joining the main line at the old station, called the 'Whitacre Junction'. Twenty seven acres of farmland were swallowed up in the construction of this junction alone. Transportation of goods and people was facilitated by the advent of the railway, opening up the community to other areas of the country. In 1842, rail services stopping at Hampton comprised five trains down to London and three trains returning each day. At this time 44 people were recorded as working on, or for the railway, including seven porters on Hampton

The Ford across the River Blythe at the bottom of Marsh Lane, showing the old packhorse bridge and the new railway viaduct.

Station. The railway brought in new enterprises; a coal wharf and a corn merchant both of which remained until the beginning of the twentieth century. The station, originally sited in what is now Old Station Road, was later moved to its present site at the 'request' of Sir Frederick Peel. The old Station House became a private residence and is now used as offices. Opposite this old site is a row of terraced cottages built for the families of the railway workers.

THE VILLAGE GROWS

All of this, and then the building of the Manor a few years later brought about further housing development in the village and increased the population once again.

Apart from the local timber business, there has been little permanent industrial activity in the village, but the development of industry and commerce in the Midland area brought about considerable social change to Hampton. At the beginning of the twentieth century there was a gradual migration of wealthy businessmen and their families moving into the rural areas. Housing styles changed to suit modern needs and the village boundaries moved outwards as this population expanded. A new school was built to house the increased intake of young children, and sporting activities including cricket, hockey, tennis and football clubs opened up. A new social structure was formed by this group of non-rural people who wanted, and could afford, the tranquillity of country life.

The most recent change in the physical structure of the village occurred in the 1960s. For the first time blocks of flats were built in three areas near the centre of the village and in the following years further tracts of land were allocated for private building. There has also been some increase in commercial activity in the village. A new office development was built on the old scrap yard near the railway, the Ring of Bells Inn was converted for office use and the old Station House is now surrounded by offices called 'Station Court'. Many residents will argue that this new influx of young people is good for the school, the shopkeepers and other businesses, and for the general livelihood and prosperity of the village. The older residents will remember the quiet, peaceful, traffic-free Warwickshire village and wonder about future changes and when will it all stop?

CHAPTER ONE

The Manor of Hampton-in-Arden

THE EARLY YEARS

Before the tenth century homesteads were self governing, but in later years, local communities were being established, and with them, organised meetings or 'Courts' held at 'Moot Mounds', or just an open space or tree that had some past religious connection. These meetings were the very beginning of the 'Court Leets' and eventually our present local Councils. They were formed from a hundred families, or ten Tithings, which was a group of ten householders, and so named 'Hundreds'. Eventually representatives of these Courts were called upon to attend 'Shire Moots', the forerunner of the County Councils and Law Courts.

The Domesday Book records ten 'Hundreds' in Warwickshire later reducing to just four. Hampton-in-Arden was situated in the 'Helmingford Hundred'. This was roughly diamond shaped with Tamworth at the top point, Birmingham at the left, Nuneaton at the right and Kenilworth at the bottom. Watling Street formed the top right hand edge running between Tamworth and Nuneaton.

The original parish, much larger than the area today, was made up of several villages and hamlets - the more notable being, Hampton, Knowle, Balsall, Chadwick (now Chadwick End), Diddington, and two which no longer appear on any modern map, Kinwalsey which lay between Meriden and Fillongley, and Nuthurst: between Hockley Heath and Lapworth. Before the Norman invasion, this 'parish' and others in the area, was owned and ruled by a Saxon lord named Leuvinus.

After the conquest this entire area was 'disposed', by King William to Geffrey de Wirce who became the first Norman Lord.

Hantone, a misspelling, possibly by a Norman French scribe, was recorded as being ten hides, with land for twenty-two ploughs, a mill worth forty pence and ten acres of meadow. A woodland area, three leagues long (approximately nine miles), by three leagues wide. In all it was worth one hundred shillings.

For reasons, which were never specified, all the lands belonging to De Wirce were later conferred upon Nigel de Albini, and then eventually passed on to his son Roger de Aubigney. At some point in his lifetime he changed his name to Roger Moubrey.

The mediaeval Manor House, now called the Moat House shown looking from the west.

A reference by John Hannett in his book Forest of Arden states that – 'One mile north west of Bickenhill Church in a field called Castle Hills, there lies the site of the castle built by either Nigel de Albini or Roger Moubray.

In the early 1100s, during the reign of King Stephen, many grants were given to build castles and holds under Royal Licence. After his death, however, Henry II laid claim to the throne and during a long period of unrest had many of the inland castles demolished, leaving only a few around the coast.

At some point, in later years, this castle ruin was rebuilt as a Manor House or 'Mansion'. An 'Inquisition', or census, taken in the fourth year of the reign of Edward I, around 1276, lists the Manor House and Park, situated in the north west of the parish, in the possession of William de Arderne

The manor was then 'enfeoffed' to Ralph de Haia, also thought to be known as Raduphus de Hamtona, a son of Turchill de Warwick, also called Turchill de Ardena.

Ralph de Haia sold the manor to Robert de Arderne who, when he became Archbishop of Liseaux passed the manor on to his two brothers Roger de Arderne and Petrus (Peter) de Arderne. Due to Peter's involvement with the Church, he eventually passed the ownership of the manor entirely to Roger.

Although exact dates are not recorded, all this transfer of ownership, between members of the Arderne family, occurred between 1086, when Geffrey de Wirce was first granted the Manor, and sometime towards the end of the Twelfth

Century. The Manor remained in the hands of the Ardernes for the next hundred years, over three further generations. After the death of Roger de Arderne, in 1173, it passed to his son William de Arderne, who also owned the Manor of Knowle. It then passed on to his son Hugo (Hugh) de Arderne, He was a man of great wealth, high in favour at Court, an Assize Judge and Governor of Warwick Prison. In 1249 he received a knighthood from King Henry III. It was Sir Hugh de Arderne who secured permission from the King to hold a weekly market, in Hampton, every Tuesday and for a three day fair to be held annually – 'on the Eve, Day and Morrow' of the feast of St. Luke, on October 18th. The historian, William Dugdale, records this weekly market, as first sited behind the blacksmith's forge. It is just possible that the blacksmith's shop, which still existed in the 1950s, opposite the Moat House, was on the same original site. At some point it was moved to a new site behind the vicarage, but what date and which vicarage is not made clear. It is thought by some that an early vicarage was situated on the present site of Church House Farm, and that the narrow pathway immediately opposite this building up to the South Porch suggests a possible connection between a vicarage and the church.

Following the death of Sir Hugh, in 1250, the manor passed to his son William de Arderne, who sided with the rebellious barons against Henry III in 1265, and was forced to flee the country. Later he submitted himself to the 'Dictum of Kenilworth', a possible form of atonement at Kenilworth Priory, and was received back into the King's favour. It was said, that he was killed in 1275 by Richard de Lifle, although this was never proven.

An indent of his lands showed – A Manor House, Two Gardens, 460 acres of land, A Meadow valued at VII.li. XII.s. (£7. 12s), Two parks, One Pool, Two Water Mills and Fishing in the River Blythe. A yearly rent from Freeholders in Kinwalsey, Diddington, Elmdon, Bickenhill, Sheldon, Nuthurst and Honiley, were all valued at LII.li. XVI.s. IV.d. (£52. 16s. 4d.)

The Arderne family had settled in Curdworth, Minworth, Kingsbury, Sutton Coldfield, and a number of other areas in north Warwickshire. Edward de Arderne, Lord of the Manor of Curdworth, was married to Mary Throckmorton of Coughton Court, another staunch Catholic family, which suffered at the hands of the crown. In 1583 he, with his son-in-law John Somerville, was implicated in what later became known as the 'Somerville Plot' to assassinate Queen Elizabeth I. They were both executed in December of that year.

At this point the manor would have passed to William's brother Richard, but he had been certified insane and so all lands and property passed to the King and were then entrusted to Bartholemew de Sudeley.

3

On the death of Richard, there being no direct heir, the manor was divided equally between his two aunts, Olivia, married to Robert le Megre, and Hawise, married to Ricardus Peche.

Olivia's half moiety passed to her daughter Amicia, wife of Sir John de Lou who then, in 1284, conveyed her half to Queen Eleanor, wife of Edward I, for an annuity of thirty pounds per year.

Hawise passed her half moiety to her son John Peche, who eventually bought back the other half from the Queen in 1299.

The manor remained in the Peche family until the reign of Richard II, passing to a grandson, also John Peche, who was 'Justice of the Gaol Deliveries' at Warwick, from 1268 to 1280.

For services to the King he was knighted in 1304 and soon afterwards was granted the post of Constable of Dover Castle and Lord Warden of the Cinque Ports. The previous holder of this post had been brought before the Royal Court for some indiscretion, but was later exonerated by the King and restored to office. Sir John died in 1376 and the manorial rights, were inherited by his son another John Peche, who held the lordship until his death in 1387. In 1411 the ownership was granted to his widow, Katherine, for the remainder of her life.

Katherine left the manor to Sir William De Mountfort, of Coleshill, her son-in-law, married to her youngest daughter Margaret. The manor then remained in the hands of the De Mountfort family until the 'Attainder', the loss of rights, of Sir Simon Mountfort for treason against King Henry VII in 1495. Once again the Lordship was forfeited to the crown.

In 1496 the manor was granted in 'Tail Male' to Richard Pudsey, equerry to King Henry VII. 'Tail Male' or 'Tale Female' was an expression given to the settlement of an Estate or Property by another party, i.e. the Crown, to one person exclusively.

Richard Pudsey died without issue and Simon Mountfort Esq. the grandson of Sir Simon, who had been attained for treason, attempted to purchase the Lordship. Unfortunately King Henry VII died before a decision could be made and so the manor remained in the hands of the Crown until 1512, when it was granted to Sir Henry Guldeford.

He also died without issue and on the death of Margaret, his wife, in 1588, the manor passed to Thomas Lysley, who held it for thirty one years, at an annual rent of fifty five pounds. It was at about this time that the Manor House, later re-named the 'Moat House', was rebuilt, and extended. The existing, late sixteenth century building had been constructed on, or near, the foundation of the earlier Manor House.

In 1572 the Manor was again granted 'in Tail Male' to Robert Dudley, Earl of Leicester, who then owned Kenilworth Castle and was at the time a favourite of Queen Elizabeth I.

Over a period of time a number of leases of land, across the Parish, were acquired by Henry Martin, the Queen's Trumpeter and a soldier of great distinction. In 1602 he attempted to purchase the entire Manor, but failed to do so.

In 1649, following the death of King Charles I, his wife Queen Henrietta carried out a complete survey of the Crown's estates. This provides us with a fascinating detailed description of the Manor House and its surrounds at that time.

The Manor House, Survey of Queen Henrietta 1649

John Loggins is shown as the immediate Tenant.

All that Capital Messuage or Manor House consisting of eight rooms below stayres and nine rooms above stayres.

Hall - with brick chimney and two glass windows 23ft. by 15ft.

Parlour - wainscoated, boarded below and covered with a 'seeling', brick chimney, two glass windows 20ft. by 10ft.

Kitchen - brick chimney, two glass windows 21ft. by 15ft.

Little room adjoining parlour, one glass window, boarded below. 9ft. by 10ft.

Little parlour with brick chimney and one glass window. 15ft. by 10ft.

Larder - one glass window. 13ft. by 10ft.

Little Buttery - one glass window, 14ft. by 11ft.

Little Buttery. 8ft. by 8ft.

Area of ground floor 1516sq.ft. all floored with earth except parlour and room adjoining.

One chamber over room adjoining Great Parlour with brick chimney and glass windows. 16ft. by 15ft.

One chamber over little parlour, one glass window and chimney. 15ft. by 10ft.

One chamber over Great Parlour, wainscotted, with chimney, two windows and 'seeling'. 15ft. by 15ft.

One chamber over part of the Hall, one window. 19ft. by 12ft.

One chamber over part of the Hall, chimney, two windows and two little closets. 23ft. by 19ft.

One chamber over part of the Kitchen, one window and 'seeling'. 17ft. by 17ft.

One chamber over part of the Butteryes, one window. 12ft. by 10ft.

One other room over part of the Kitchen, one chimney, one window and 'seeling' 16ft. by 14ft. One small chamber over part of the Butteryes, one window, old 'seeling' Garret over some part of chambers.

Area of upper floor 1833sq. ft.

Total living area 3500sq.ft.

One room adjoining the house where they make Malt and a little stable under one roof with chamber over 33ft. by 15ft.

The house and above room covered with tile.

One barn, three bays and a porch, covered with tile 72ft. by 18ft.

Little stable at one end of barn and cart house at the other end.

One other barn consisting of five bays with two cow houses at each end, one on each side. Half the length covered in thatch. 94ft. by 22ft.

One large yard, one little courtyard, one orchard with apple trees, one garden plot.

Which said Manor House with the Scite is thereof - Bounded with the Church yard on the East, in part upon a lane called Salters Lane on the West, a close called The Walke on the North and a streete called Hampton Streete on the South, containing three acres.

The earliest surviving Court Book of the Manor of Hampton lists the succession of holders of the lordship and the stewards who held the living and maintained the estate on their behalf.

Date	Lord of the Manor	Steward
1661	Queen Henrietta Maria. (wife of Charles I.)	John Knight
1678	Robert Vyner. (Knt. & Bart)	Francis Ede
1700	Henry Parker (Bart)	William Knight
1720	Ralph Sheldon & Nathaniel Piggott	Fettisplace Nott
1725	Henry Parker (Bart)	Joseph Hunt
1736	Sir Henry John Parker (Bart)	Joseph Hunt
1758	Sir John Hunt (Bart)	Illedge Maddox
1759	Sir John Hunt (Bart)	James Baine
1760-1798	Sir Henry Gough (later Lord Calthorpe)	Anthony Mainwaring (to 1787)
		Henry Geast (to 1792)

Then followed by Lady Calthorpe until the son George, Lord Calthorpe became of age in 1812.

Richard Geast (to 1796)
William Bedfor (to 1813)
John Yeen (to 1833)

Over these years, all but four of the Court meetings, or 'Leets' were held at the Stonebridge Inn, the proprietor being - Elizabeth Proctor (Widow). The remaining four were held at the White Lion Inn, owned by William Smith.

THE MANOR IN THE 19TH AND 20TH CENTURIES

On the death of George III we have George IV as Lord of the Manor. But presumably he decided that Hampton was a bit out of the way and perhaps needed some money. In any event we have an early example of privatisation. He put the Manor up for sale in London on November 23rd 1823. A map drawn in 1812 and currently held at the Public Record Office in London seems to have been used as the basis for the sale. The Manor estate is not very different from the description of the Manor land in 1649. The 1812 map appears to have been drawn following the Enclosure Act of 1810 which was the start of the significant change in land ownership in the parish. The Manor was bought by Abraham Spooner Lillingston, who lived at Elmdon Hall.

A Spy cartoon of Sir Frederick Peel, originally published in Vanity Fair.

The map of 1812 shows that Hampton Manor estate consisted of three farms plus some small pieces of land and woods let to others. The farms are Castle Hills farm run by George Repton, Home farm run by Joseph Crockett and Hampton Hall farm run by William Osborne. Hampton Hall farm was based on the old Manor House, now known as the Moat House.

On the death of Abraham Lillingston the Earl of Aylesford bought Castle Hills farm. Sir Robert Peel, father of Frederick and the famous prime minister, buying Home farm. And Abraham Spooner Lillingston's son Isaac William retained Hampton Hall farm and the Lordship of the Manor.

One of the most important dates as far as who owned what is concerned is 1841 when the Hampton Tithe award was made. This lists every field in the parish stating who owned it, who used it, how large it was in acres, roods and perches and the tithes that had to be paid. Like many other parishes there were two tithes, the lesser tithe which was paid to the vicar and the greater tithe which was normally paid to the rector. In Hampton's case the rectorial tithes had been granted to the Lord Leycester Hospital in Warwick. According to this list Isaac Lillingston owned the Moat house and the associated farm but did not live there. Sir Robert Peel owned 422 acres in the village and the Earl of Aylesford owned 699 acres.

Later in the year Hampton Hall farm was sold, with Sir Robert Peel buying the manor house and some land. However the Earl of Aylesford also increased his holding of land in the parish.

The sale of 1823 was not the first time that a Peel had acquired some land in the parish. The first contact that we know of was in 1814 when some land was purchased by a Sir Robert Peel. This would have been the Sir Robert Peel, the first baronet. The well known Sir Robert Peel was the second baronet.

This was at the time when the Enclosure Acts were changing the face of the countryside. The Enclosure Act for Hampton was passed in 1805 and implemented in 1812. In the Court Roll dated 19th July 1814 it is reported that *"land allotted by the Commission to Elizabeth Moland (Plot 146) is stated as - to the use of Sir Robert Peel, Baronet, his heirs and successors, at the will of the Lord according to the custom of the said Manor. And also to this Court came Sir Robert Peel, Baronet, in his own proper person and in open court prayed to be admitted Tenant to the aforesaid premises with the appurtenancies to whom the said Lord of the Manor by his Steward aforesaid at this Court hath granted seizan thereof by the Rod."* This meeting of the Court was yet another held *"at the House of William Smith called the White Lion."*

Sir Robert Peel paid a fine of £9 for the transfer. In fact a fine had a different meaning in those days, it was just the name given to the payment by an incoming tenant to the manorial lord.

In view of the influence that the Peels had on Hampton some background to the family is worth noting. Sir Robert Peel, the first baronet, was born in Lancashire in 1750. His family had moved from Yorkshire in the 17th century to Blackburn where his father, also called Robert Peel, had founded the family fortunes when he set up, in partnership with two others a calico-printing firm. He had seven sons and Robert, who became the first baronet was the second of these. At the age of 23 Robert entered the family business. He was a believer in progress and wanted to implement some of the mechanical improvements invented by Arkwright and Hargreaves. He decided to do this away from Lancashire, probably because he feared that doing it at home, as it were, would invoke the jealousy of the handloom weavers. He therefore moved a branch of the business to Tamworth in Staffordshire and bought a large estate nearby where he built Drayton Manor. As well as being a businessman he also became M.P. for

Tamworth in 1790 and was made a baronet in 1800. At one point he employed 15,000 people and the firm donated £10,000 to help oppose the French Revolution. Presumably that is where the baronetcy came from.

His eldest son, and second baronet, was born in Bury in Lancashire in 1788 and was the famous Prime Minister.

As mentioned he bought the Manor Estate from Isaac William Lillingston in 1841. He bought several parcels of land in the next few years but unfortunately he was thrown from his horse whilst riding up Constitution Hill on 29th June 1850 sustaining injuries from which he died three days later.

He had five sons and two daughters. Sir Frederick Peel was his second son and was born in 1823. It was the youngest son, Arthur Wellesley Peel, who became Speaker of the House of Commons and who was created Viscount Peel on his retirement in 1895. Thus Sir Frederick is not a direct ancestor of the present Lord Peel. It is interesting to note that not only were Sir Frederick's father and grandfather M.P.s but he also had three uncles and two brothers who were M.P.s. It is no surprise that Frederick became an M.P. Westminster must have seemed like a second family home.

On the unexpected death of the famous Sir Robert Peel, the eldest son, Sir Robert Peel, was left the family's main country estate at Drayton Park, and the will continues,

"I leave my freehold Estate consisting of about one hundred and fifty three acres situate in the parish of Sutton Coldfield and all that the Manor or reputed Manor or Lordship of Hampton in Arden in the parish of Hampton in Arden or in any parishes adjoining to my son Frederick Peel".

Frederick Peel was educated at Harrow and Trinity College, Cambridge, he became a student at the Inner Temple and was called to the Bar in February 1849. In the same month he entered the House of Commons, being returned unopposed as Liberal member for Leominster.

In 1851 he became Under-Secretary of State for the Colonies. In the general election of 1852 he successfully contested Bury. In 1855 Lord Palmerston appointed him Under-Secretary for War. In 1857 he lost his seat for Bury and resigned office, being made a Privy Councillor for his services. On being re-elected for Bury in 1859 he became Financial Secretary to the Treasury, a post he held until 1865, when he was again defeated at Bury. He failed to become elected for south-east Lancashire in 1868 and that was the end of his political career. He was created K.C.M.G. in 1869.

In 1873, on the passing of the Regulation of Railways Act, Peel was appointed a member of the Railway and Canal Commission, on which he served until his death. The tribunal was a court of arbitration to settle disagreements between railways and their customers, which lay beyond the scope of ordinary litigation. As senior commissioner Peel became the most influential member of the tribunal.

Frederick Peel was 27 when his father died and left him Hampton Manor. Peel began the building of the manor house in about 1852. John Hannett, writing in 1863, says of the Manor House *"Built by, and the residence of, the Right Honourable Frederick Peel, the present Lord of the manor. The edifice, standing on a commanding eminence, west of the old manor-place, is built in the castellated style, from designs by - Giles, esq. of Derby"*. He goes on to say that *"when the trees and shrubs which fill the gardens and surrounding plantations have attained a larger growth, they will materially contribute to the interest and beauty of the locality"*. I think that they have done that and I hope that Sir Frederick did get a feel of what he had created.

This was before the coming of W. Eden Nesfield who was responsible for "improving the manor". He had originally been commissioned to carry out the restoration of the parish church but stayed to carry out a number of commissions for Sir Frederick Peel. The most important of these as far as the Manor House was concerned was the Clock Tower, erected in 1872. But he was also responsible for a number of buildings which significantly changed the face of the village.

At the time that Frederick Peel was building the present Manor House he appears to have exchanged some land with the Earl of Aylesford. It would appear that this was how he acquired the land where the recreation ground and spinney are now. Presumably he wanted a have a private road and entrance to the then Railway Station, then situated down the present Old Station Road.

In view of the several coats of arms that he used on his buildings it is worth commenting on them.

The Peel family coat of arms shows a bee on the upper part of the shield, and three sets of three arrows on the bottom half. A second son had these modified by the addition of a crescent placed top centre. You can see this coat of arms carved high on the wall at the foot of the stairs inside the Manor House as you go through to the foyer. They are also carved on the side of the lodge at the foot of the drive. When someone married it was quite common to place the arms of the husband and wife side by side on a shield; this was known as impalement, and generally signifies a temporary or non-hereditary combination of arms. Normally the mark added to indicate say a second son is dropped when this happens. You can see two examples of this that Sir Frederick had carved. The first is on the pargeted cottages which were built in 1868. In this case we have the Peel coat of arms on the left and on the right we have three mussels. These are from the Shelley coat of arms (his first wife

The Manor and it garden in its heyday.

was Elizabeth Shelley). There is another combination of arms over the building now used as an office. This has the date 1892 and the Peel coat of arms is combined with an eagle from the coat of arms from his second wife's family, the Pleydell-Bouveries.

The other embellishment that you will see both inside and outside the house is the crossed initials F.P. and E.P., Frederick and Elizabeth. The most obvious ones are over the fireplaces in the drawing room. There are also some straight F.P. initials in various places.

Sir Frederick Peel played a full part in village life, albeit a fairly autocratic one. He was a generous supporter of the church most of which is detailed in the Rev. Adam's book on the history of Hampton. One quite poignant gift is that a piece of land, about half an acre, which formerly formed part of the moat surrounding the old manor house lying to the west of the church tower. He had it filled in and gave to the church in order to extend the churchyard. Sir Frederick is buried in that piece of land.

There is one additional story which is mentioned by Mr Adams. It was related by Miss King in her talk to the Women's Institute in 1935. She quotes the village postmaster, Robert Thompson, as saying that the Post Office was originally in what is now the corner shop. But Sir Frederick did not approve; it was far from the right and proper place. So he had it moved across the road to what we now know as the Old Post Office. This is fully consistent with the records that we have of the village postmaster.

Sir Frederick Peel died in London on 6th June 1906 and was buried at Hampton-in-Arden. He was survived by his second wife, Janet, Lady Peel who was left a life interest in Hampton Manor and although she did not die until 1925 she discontinued living in the Manor well before that and it was put up for sale in 1919.

In Sir Frederick Peel's obituary in the Times the comment is made that, *"After the death of Palmerston, he found himself ill-suited to the more democratic temper of parliamentary life. He had his father's judicial mind and cautious, equable temper, but his reticence and aloofness militated against his success in public life."*

The Manor was sold in 1919 and was purchased by James Rollason, a manufacturer from Birmingham. He worked in the family firm, Abel Rollason and Sons Ltd.

When he died in 1936, his wife, Grace Eveline Rollason, was given the option to lease the Manor at a peppercorn rent for the rest of her life. His will continues to say that once his wife no longer requires it, Hampton Manor and grounds should, before any sale, be offered to his son Melvyn Howard Rollason at the price of £22,500. If he declines then it should be offered to his other son, Neville Howard Rollason and failing that to his daughter, Mildred Howard Rollason. None of them were interested in buying the estate.

The estate was put up for sale therefore in 1952 on the death of Mrs Rollason and the next phase in the history of the Manor began. The Manor House and 62 acres of land were bought by Alfred and Hilda Jacobs, husband and wife, and they founded Hampton Manor Homes. Mr Jacobs was an engineer and they both originally came from Birmingham. They had lived a large part of their married life in the village, at a bungalow called "Goodrest" in Old Station Road. This is now called "Brunswick House". But in 1952 they had moved and were living in the Manor House, now demolished, in Berkswell. They had three children, Alice Jean who died in 1983, Edward, known as Teddy, and Brenda, known as Lindy, now Mrs Wood.

Teddy was born with Down's Syndrome and was cared for at Sunfield Children's Home at Clent in Worcestershire. He was very happy there but the children had to leave at the age of sixteen. Mr and Mrs Jacobs did not want their child and others like him to be hospitalised when they left the Sunfield Home. They wanted him to be in a home that would continue his education and personal development.

It was with this in mind that they bought Hampton Manor in 1952. The Manor having been put up for sale following the death of Mrs Rollason who had lived there on her own since the death of her husband in 1936.

In those days children were segregated by sex and the people who Mr and Mrs Jacobs found who were prepared to run the home particularly wanted to look after girls. Mr and Mrs Jacobs were not trained so could not do it themselves. Unfortunately Teddy Jacobs died at Sunfield in 1951 and Hampton Manor Home was opened in 1952. The home is registered for 32 people.

It should be remembered that in 1952 there was no help from the State nor were then any inspections.

Sunfield Children's Home and Hampton Manor Home were founded on the philosophies of Rudolph Steiner (1861-1925). His teachings were complex and avant-garde for their day, but Hampton Manor has steadfastly worked using Steiner's principles which lay down that everyone has a part to play in society and everyone can make achievements, enjoy life and in doing so realise their own capabilities.

Mr and Mrs Jacobs retired from a their business life and came to manage and help run Hampton Manor Home. The residents were taught weaving by Mrs Jacobs and the looms used are still around but although they still have the space they have no teacher.

The Jacobs sold everything and took out a mortgage in order to buy the Manor with its 46 acres of ground for £19,200. Initially they just had their own furniture with which to furnish the building. They started out living in a room over the front door so they could hear when visitors called and could then nip down and open it.

At the time of the purchase of the Manor the stables were uninhabitable but Mr and Mrs Jacobs renovated them and then moved out of the Manor to live there. The Stables, now Manor Cottage, were subsequently occupied by Mr and Mrs Burgess, the parents of one of the residents who wanted to live near their daughter. Later the daughter moved to the West Country and Mr and Mrs Burgess left.

In the early 1970s it became apparent that a hall was necessary to accommodate meetings of parents, production of plays etc. In order to raise sufficient money to build a hall some land adjacent to the High Street was sold to a developer. This is the site of the four bungalows, numbers 15 to 21 the High Street. The Gardener's Lodge was also sold to its present owners and is better known as the Lodge, in the High Street.

The Station Lodge and the land associated with it was sold to the Fentham Trust for a peppercorn figure in the 1960s and is now better known as Fentham Green.

In 1971 Mrs Jacobs died and in 1974 John and Lindy Wood took over the running of the Homes. Mr Jacobs died in 1976.

In 1984 the Government passed the Social Care Act which has brought many changes in its wake. The local Department of Social Services were given powers to inspect, review and initiate changes in care pattern consistent with the Act. This had previously been the responsibility of the placing authority. The Act was the first step in reducing the number of beds per room. This meant a significant change in the accommodation upstairs which in turn meant that the drainage system was inadequate. The necessary changes to the sewage system were carried out in 1987 with a change in direction of the outlet. The Manor is still on a septic tank but the liquids do go into the sewerage system. New electricity cables had to be installed and the roof has had to be renewed – it is mainly lead and slate. Apart from this work the Manor is basically the same building that was originally built in 1855.

CHAPTER TWO

Village Churches

THE PARISH CHURCH OF ST. MARY AND ST. BARTHOLOMEW

The history of the Parish Church is well covered in the book by the Reverend J.C. Adams "Hampton in Arden, A Warwickshire Village". It was felt the church should not be excluded from this book so that a brief history of the Parish Church is included.

The Domesday Survey of 1086 is the earliest record of the village church, probably at that time a small wooden thatched building serving as a place of worship and as a communal hall. This was replaced in about 1130 by a stone structure which is now the chancel and still contains traces of its Norman origins.

As demand for space grew over the next fifty years the main nave was added, together with the south aisle and later the north aisle. The tower was completed in the late fifteenth century and has an uncommon semi-circular stair turret lining to its outer wall.

In the chancel there is a fifteenth century stained glass window, ninety tiles in the floor from the 14th and 15th centuries and also the remains of 13th century stone coffin lids. The earliest known burial under the chancel floor is that of Sir John Peche, who died in 1338, buried with 30 other bodies and on the south wall is a heart tomb.

Outside the church on the south wall is a scratch dial or Mass dial from the 14th century. The churchyard cross, originally built in 1450 and 22 feet high, is situated east of the east window. Only the base remains.

In 1553 there were three bells in the belfry. Re-casting and additions took place in 1629 and in 1634, but it is believed that they all were destroyed, together with the steeple in a violent storm of 1643. The parishioners were instructed to rebuild the steeple on a more modest scale but it was never rebuilt.

Six new bells were cast in 1725 by Joseph Smith of Edgbaston, these being sold to the parish of Nether Whitacre in 1975. They were replaced by the present set of bells acquired in 1976 from the church at Miles Platting.

In the nave the Royal Coat of Arms, situated at the west end of the north wall dates from 1717. Eight hundred years of history are portrayed in a chronological chart hanging on the south wall, and until the 1870s there were box pews throughout. Above the arcading are replicas of six Manorial Arms of Lordships, being those of de la Bere, Peche, Allain, Bradstone and Say of Richards Castle and lastly Sir Frederick Peel.

In 1802 there is the first account of restoration. This was not a major restoration but was work undertaken as a result of a report which stated "that the pulpit and reading desk together with all the seats and pews and sitting places within the church are in a ruinous and dilapidated state and are unfit for the decent accommodation of parishioners". At this time it was felt that there were not enough seats in the church and the gallery at the west end was enlarged to hold thirty seats. The pews were of the "box" variety and were six feet wide and three feet nine inches high and each had a door. It was estimated that the total number of people who could be seated in the church was 462 including thirty in the gallery and thirty six in the chancel. The new pulpit was of the three-decker type and the preachers stand, which stood to the north of the middle pillar of the south aisle, was reached by a small winding stair.

In 1839 another addition was made: an organ was presented to the church by Isaac William Lillingstone. He was quoted as being of Loch Alsh in Scotland but

The Parish Church undergoing restoration in 1872.

The Parish Church from the High Street as it looked during the first half of the 20th Century.

he was also the Lord of the Manor of Elmdon and lived in Elmdon Hall. There was concern that the gallery was not strong enough to take the organ and it was eventually decided to prepare a gallery to carry the instrument and at the same time the gallery was made big enough to accommodate about one hundred Sunday School children. The first drain was also built around the church in 1839.

In 1866 Theodore Morris, who had been a curate under his father Joseph Morris, became the vicar. Presumably he was concerned about the fabric of the church which was in poor condition and a survey was requested and carried out by the architect, William Eden Nesfield in 1866. His initial report was updated in 1869 at the same time that the vicar instituted the Parish Magazine and started the Church Restoration Fund.

W. Eden Nesfield's report did not make pleasant reading. Among the things he said was that the south wall of the chancel was 9-10 inches out of the perpendicular and was still giving way. The result was that he recommended a series of actions including the taking down of the aforesaid south wall and rebuilding it. A photograph taken during the restoration in 1878 shows the building minus this wall and its roof. Not only did Nesfield recommend a course of restoration he went further and recommended the rebuilding of the church spire. This caused a considerable amount of controversy and was dropped.

The Victorian Vicarage.

Since then a number of improvements have been carried out including a new clock for the tower in 1886 and later a new organ. The tower was restored in 1907 and the peal of bells rehung.

Between the nave and the chancel is a Rood Screen, donated in 1910 by Lady Janet Peel, widow of Sir Frederick Peel. The east window of the chancel was given by Sir Frederick Peel in 1903 in memory of his first wife, Emily.

The present Village Chronicle was started as the Parish Magazine in 1869. Over the years it has changed its name several times. In 1945 it was the Church Chronicle but in that year it changed its name to be the Church and Village Chronicle so that its audience increased. The new magazine had regular contributions from the Congregational Church as well as other village organisations.

THE CONGREGATIONAL CHURCH

As with the parish church the congregational church is a separate chapter in the village history produced by J. C. Adams. On November 28th 1838 the Congregational Church was officially opened although at that time it was known as the Providence Chapel. This opening was the result of a growing movement of non-conformity in the village. In 1662, the curate of Hampton-in-Arden, Mr Packwood, was accused of recusancy, i.e. he refused to conform to the laws and practices of the Established Church and was ejected from the living. He was related by marriage to

George Fentham who was also known to have non-conformist sympathies. Among the first list of members of the Congregational Church the name James Fentham occurs. But Mr Packwood was not the first or the last to be accused of recusancy.

At the beginning of the nineteenth century a small band of people met for worship on a Sunday in a cottage and a Sunday School for children was also held but where is not known.

The first record of the building of the chapel refers to the acquisition of a small parcel of pasture known as Butt Close adjoining the George Fentham Boys School and having frontage to a rough track used by the school boys known as Narrow Walk. This piece of land belonged to Louisa Moore, a widowed daughter of William Eborall of Balsall Street. When William Eborall died, he left his estate in trust to his housekeeper, Mary Marks, and on her death, it was to be divided between his three daughters, Susannah, Louisa and Caroline. Mary died in 1830. Susannah had died in 1825, Caroline then died in 1831 so the whole estate came to Louisa.

Shortly after this Louisa married a second husband, Edmund Simonds, who had come to the village from Liverpool where he had been a member of the Great George Street Congregational Church. Why he came to Hampton is not known but come he did and he built the house in Marsh Lane which has since been transformed into the Fentham Club but was originally known as *"the Beeches"*.

The site, known as Butt Close, was transferred from the Eborall Estate for the sum of £10 10s. It was bought for the purpose of erecting a chapel or meeting house thereon for the use of a society or community of protestant dissenters from the Church of England of the Congregational order or persuasion commonly called Independents, in the neighbourhood of Hampton-in-Arden. It was to be built with money collected and raised by people of this persuasion for the public worship and service of Almighty God.

The Congregational Chapel was affected by the formation of the United Reformed Church on October 5th 1972. This was a union between the Congregational Church in England and Wales and the Presbyterian Church of England. The building was purchased by the Fentham Trust and the top room was used as a temporary class room. Later on it was leased to the West Midlands Federation of Women's Institutes. The organ from the Congregational Church was given by the Fentham Trust to the Chelmsley Wood Christadelphian Ecclesia in 1976.

THE COPTIC CHURCH
The Congregational Church was sold to the Coptic Church in 1984 since 1985 has been known as the Coptic Orthodox Church of St. Mary and St. Anthony.

19

CHAPTER THREE

Farms and Farming

INTRODUCTION

Before Hampton-in-Arden appeared as a place name on any map or someone had the idea of forming a village settlement in the early tenth century, small groups of wandering Saxons had penetrated this forest area of the Midlands. This early population of families was responsible for a collection of isolated hamlets sited in woodland clearings each producing their own crops, and so forming the first farms.

By 1086, the family groups had grown and merged, larger areas of the forest had been cleared and the parish, now controlled by a Norman lord, extended over an area of 11,500 acres compared with 2,500 acres today. Over the centuries, the parish of Hampton was to change dramatically, this brought about by three major human influences - settlement, enclosure and industrialisation.

As larger areas were cleared for the production of crops to feed the increasing population, new methods of collective farming were introduced in the form of an Open Field System, developing into a Four Field System of crop rotation and animal grazing. This system continued until the beginning of the nineteenth century when Parliament implemented the Enclosure Act, resulting in the creation of a new landscape of small regular fields bounded by hedgerows and fences, owned privately, or leased from the Lord of the Manor.

Over many years the pathways, naturally formed by regular use between the original hamlets, became farm tracks more suited for carts carrying local produce. Eventually as farming became more efficient, and with the growing population in towns and cities requiring a regular supply of farm produce into the markets, the surface of these tracks was gradually improved, and so began to form the structure of the roads as we know them today. These roads, together with the eventual construction of the Grand Union Canal on the western boundary of the parish, and the railway across the north-east of the village, brought about considerable change to the landscape, the structure and prosperity of the village of Hampton-in-Arden.

The River Blythe is slow moving, having a gradient of only one in seven hundred over its 27 mile length with a wide open flood plain which collects well over half the drainage of the area. The first recorded attempt to secure this flood plain was made in 1813 by Lord Aylesford. At a cost of one hundred pounds per mile, the river was successfully dredged and widened, preventing further silting, and so improving the surrounding meadowland for farming.

The landscape within the parish is subdued in relief, rising sharply up into the village from the west with a longer and more gradual gradient to the north and east. The boundaries are formed, almost entirely by natural waterways. The Blythe forms the eastern boundary separating the village from Meriden, but the Grand Union Canal borders Solihull to the west. Two tributaries of the Blythe, called Shadow Brook and Low Brook, form the boundaries between Bickenhill and Elmdon to the north and in the south, with another small tributary meeting the Blythe near the Packhorse Bridge.

PRE-ENCLOSURE LANDSCAPE

At the beginning of the eighteenth century the rural landscape of Hampton-in-Arden was still far from assuming its present likeness. The Open Field system had changed very little since the thirteenth century with arable fields, meadows and great tracts of common pasture, much of it still covered by gorse and furze. Before the act of enclosure this form of agriculture was predominant over all of lowland Britain, a vast area from the Hampshire and Sussex coast, northwards through central England to the east coast from The Wash to Newcastle. Open Field husbandry signified the cooperative manner in which the inhabitants of a township subdivided and tilled their arable, meadow and pasture land, based upon production for subsistence within a village community. This was, essentially, a self-contained social and economic organisation growing crops for very local use and not market orientated. Generally, no money changed hands, the produce was paid for in kind or by services.

A tripartite division of all village land existed for agriculture separated into arable, meadow and pasture. The farmer needed arable land to produce wheat and rye for his bread, and barley for his livestock, and the meadows to grow a sufficient quantity of hay for the winter feeding of his cattle, in a time long before the introduction of root crops and manufactured winter feeds.

In 1652, Hampton was divided into four common fields - Shirley Field, Mill Field, Innfield and Innedge Field, surrounding the village in an arc, from the east side across the north to the west. Meadow land was also fairly abundant, particularly Lea Meadow and Twelve Acre Meadow, situated in the south-east of the parish in the flood plain of the River Blythe. By 1773, Innedge Field had ceased to exist since a good deal of unlawful enclosure had already taken place.

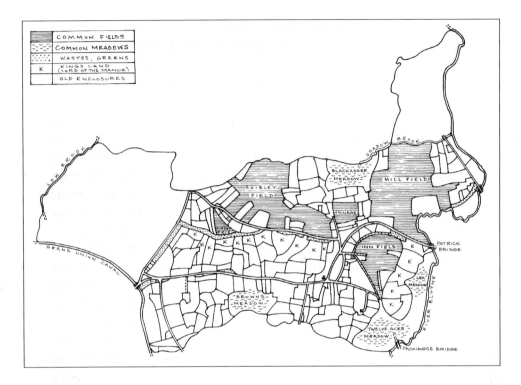

An early map of Hampton Parish showing the common fields and meadows before the implementation of the Enclosure Act in 1805.

Many of the open commons or wastes were inhabited by squatters, who built huts of mud and thatch, paying no rents or taxes. As far back as 1607 it was reported that, *"On a place of assembly called Hampton Field a considerable company of rioters calling themselves the Diggers of Warwickshire threw down some enclosures and called upon all other Diggers to follow suit"*. In total there were over 8,000 rioters in areas of Warwickshire who were eventually disbanded by the Military.

SUBDIVISION OF THE COMMON FIELDS

The open fields were subdivided, more or less, into rectangular areas (furlongs) each made up of a number of long narrow strips. Within a three or four field system, every farmer generally had strips in each field. The open field system necessitated regulations concerning the choice of arable crops grown and the periods of grazing. Every proprietor had to grow the same crop as his neighbour and the sowing and harvesting dates of this crop officially arranged. The common meadows had to be cleared of livestock by Candlemas (February 2nd) and the Peas Field cleared by St.

Matthews Day (February 24th). After the crops had been harvested, generally around Lammas Day (August 1st) and the grain harvest gathered in by late September, the land became common pasture once again, for grazing until the next agreed sowing time. This timetable was closely monitored by the Court Baron, who imposed fines on offenders ranging between two shillings and sixpence and ten shillings.

The Bye Laws also dictated that, "No person shall stock in the Common Fields and meadows more than four horses, six cows and sixteen sheep to a Yard Land, sometimes known as a Virgate, which varied about twenty acres. This was to prevent over stocking leading to the deterioration of livestock and disease. The penalty for this was a fine by the court of 39s 11d. All sheep or cattle had to be branded by the owner before being turned out onto the pastures. This was important for easy identification of ownership and as a check on individuals exceeding their quota.

These Bye-Laws illustrate the rigid regulations that were enforced upon community farming. A stable system was essential for the very survival of the entire settlement. Cattle and sheep grazing was controlled by the sowing and harvesting dates of crops under cultivation. Meadowlands were similarly controlled for the provision of a hay harvest to last the cattle through the winter period.

The four open fields dominated the landscape in Hampton-in-Arden, covering some 600 acres of the parish. There would have been few boundaries formed by hedges and trees, with the possible exception of land owned by the Lord of the Manor and other Freeholders. Very few tracks existed across the rural landscape at this time compared with the profusion of pathways that were required for access to the later enclosed areas. Prior to the nineteenth century the occupation of almost all the inhabitants of the village was connected with the land. Inventories taken between 1550 and 1648 show that out of 59 inhabitants of Hampton only nine kept no farm animals and four of these were poor widows. Over this period the use of oxen for ploughing steadily declined and they were replaced by horses. During the late sixteenth and early seventeenth centuries there was a general decline in animal husbandry. Animal herds were never very large in Hampton parish, Lady Alice Sawaye is shown in one inventory as owning 36 cattle, by far the largest number during this period, and the largest single flock of sheep, numbering 39, was owned by the Reverend Richard Baynton in 1565.

An increasing number of inventories produced show a general pattern of the smaller landowners, swinging towards arable farming. Crop values increased, possibly due to the increased need by the growing town populations. Inventories taken between 1550 and 1600 showed crops valued at seventy seven pounds, with a similar quantity of crops, recorded between 1600 and 1648, valued at over two hundred pounds.

THE EFFECTS OF ENCLOSURE

The Enclosure Act was passed by Parliament in 1805 but due to the large number of smallholdings involved it was not finally implemented until 1812. Hampton-in-Arden was not altogether without enclosed fields prior to this date, some areas of the Crown Estate had already been enclosed by trees and hedgerows and other more wealthy landowners had also succeeded in enclosing their properties. This was an indication that farmers were recognising the disadvantages of the open field system, and the strict regulations that were applied to them, and preferred to control their land in their own way and to their own timetable.

Husbandry began to be studied more scientifically, and two new factors appeared which could never have been applied to the old open field system. Root crops could now be grown without the fear of being damaged by livestock, and a system of cheap underground drainage was introduced, which suited the wet clay soil of the north Warwickshire areas.

In Hampton-in-Arden 26 local farmers petitioned and were allotted plots of land. The Earl of Aylesford was allotted 22 plots, covering an area of 27 acres. The King, who was Lord of the Manor at that time, was awarded 163 acres, and was also entitled to one twentieth of the wastelands left after the public and private roads had been set out. This bonus of land went towards the costs incurred by the Crown, for the execution of the Enclosure Act. Other large allocations of land were made to John Wedge, Ann England Fowler, George Tandy, James Tandy, Edward Barford and Richard Astley.

The conversion of the open fields into enclosed farming areas brought into being hedgerows, trees, fences and ditches to help drainage, all of which brought considerable change to the pattern of the rural landscape. The few existing main roads remained unaffected by the Act and new public roads were created to provide easier access to the new enclosed areas. Marsh Lane was extended through the original meadow land to Packhorse Bridge and a new road constructed, joining the main road through Hampton to the Hamlet of Diddington. It cut through the former Mill Field, originally called Millfield Road, now Diddington Lane. Thirteen more private carriage, or drift roads, and a considerable number of footpaths were created by the landowners, who had the responsibility of maintenance and repair. Farm work increased and there was no appearance of any great exodus to the new industrial areas. This fact is reflected in the population statistics for Hampton across the first half of the nineteenth century, which rose from four hundred and six to five hundred and fifty eight.

THE MODERN FARMING LANDSCAPE

Farmland has changed considerably in character over the last century. With the increase and improvement of farm mechanisation the smaller fields of the early enclosures have become inefficient. To combat this, many farmers have removed hedges and trees, and filled in the ditches to turn the fields into larger, more economic units. This is not a return to the old open field system but is a change brought about by new style farming and the greater need by the public for farm - produced food.

The character of farms has also changed; whereas in previous centuries smallholdings were the common practice, today there is the tendency for fewer and larger farms. The average farm acreage today is 205 acres compared with 77 in 1851. The study of individual farms, in Hampton-in-Arden in the nineteen sixties, reveals a fairly equal balance of land use, 45 per cent of arable cultivation and 55 per cent of pasture, including meadow and rotational grass. In the early nineteen seventies there were nine farms exclusively within the parish and three in the neighbouring parishes of Bickenhill and Meriden.

CHAPTER FOUR

Mills around the Parish

INTRODUCTION

The Romans may have attempted to build the first watermills in Britain but it was the Saxons who were eventually responsible for the introduction of a large number of mills. The first reference to a mill is recorded in a document dated 762 AD, in which King Ethelbert of Kent grants the use of a mill to a monastery in the district of Cert, near Dover.

In 1086 William I commissioned a survey of England, recorded in the Domesday Book, which mentions the existence of 5,264 mills. These are not defined by type and could be a mixture of water, hand or animal driven mills. The term 'mill' does not refer to the building or structure, but to the actual millstone, so a building containing two sets of millstones would be listed in the survey as two mills. Before the 12th century the majority of mills were driven by water, and just a few propelled by hand or by animals. At about this time, crusaders returning from the Middle East brought back stories of mills powered by wind, invented by the Arabs in the 7th century, and so introduced them into Britain. These were mainly used in areas where water was not available, or as a standby alongside the watermill, either when a consistent supply of water could not be relied upon, or during the replacement or re-cutting of the water powered millstones. With the continual vibration and general wear and tear no mill structure was expected to have a working life of more than 200 years. Up to 1919 there were still 350 working windmills in this country.

During the 14th and 15th centuries a mill was deemed to belong to the owner of the land upon which it was built, in many cases the Lord of the Manor, and so it became a valuable source of income. Every owner possessed 'Soke Rights' by which he could expect everyone living in the manor to send their corn to his mill to be ground. Many of the mills were rented, but some were purchased, and it was customary for the miller to take a portion, usually a sixteenth, of the flour as payment for his work.

The produce from the mill was determined by the type of millstone installed. French burr stones were favoured for corn milling, giving the finest flour. These

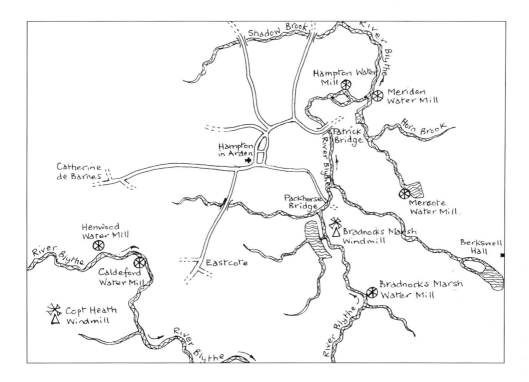

The River Blythe Waterways - Water Mills and Windmills of Hampton-in-Arden.

stones were the most expensive that could be obtained and during the Napoleonic wars were difficult to find. A few were still imported and some even smuggled into the country. French stones are easily recognised; they are not a single cut stone, but are made from straight-sided pieces, slotted together like a jigsaw within a shrunk fit iron band, and usually fitted with adjustable balance weights. Blue or 'Cullin' stones, originally imported from Cologne were used for general purpose grinding, while 'Peak' or 'Millstone Grit' stones from the Peak District of Derbyshire were mainly used for the grinding of animal feed.

The facing and balancing of millstones was a highly skilled job, carried out by millwrights who also did repairs to the rest of the mill machinery, including water wheels and windmill sails, or sweeps. Records show that much of this work was carried out by a firm called Summers, of Tanworth-in-Arden. Starting in 1814 as a blacksmith, Robert Summers moved into the millwright's business in 1833. His main competitors were Ball and Horton, later Ball Brothers of Stratford upon Avon, William Glover of Warwick, and Edward White of Redditch. Job Toon of Atherstone, operated mainly in the north of Warwickshire.

The millstone mounted on the wall of the gateway into The Elms, near the corner of Fentham Road and Marsh Lane, Hampton is a millstone grit running stone of 1.17metre diameter. It was fitted into the wall by Fred Jones, the owner of The Elms, in the 1960s. It was originally used, with the grinding face uppermost, as the doorstep of West End Cottage, on the corner of Solihull Road and Eastcote Lane. The stone has a number 1713 and a cross, carved into the upper face. Could this have been blessed at the time it was installed? If the number is a date then this stone pre-dates any known mill in the Hampton area. There are other remnants of millstones still in existence, forming a set of steps originally in the garden of The Beeches, and which at one time were the steps leading down to the bowling green.

THE BRADNOCKS MARSH MILLS, THE WATER MILL

In 1086 the Domesday Book records a mill in Barston, valued at four shillings. The exact position of this mill is not known but it may possibly have been the mill shown at Bradnocks Marsh on the 1722-25 survey map of Warwickshire produced by Henry Beighton. As there are two other mill sites in Barston, nearer the village centre, we cannot be sure.

Two mills were recorded at Barston in 1185, and in 1588 the manor is documented as having two watermills, but it is not known if these were on the same sites. The Tythe map of 1840 shows 2 Mill Meadows, 3 Mill Fields and 2 Mill Field Meadows at three sites along the bank of the river.

In 1838, the trustees of the William Ford Charity in Coventry leased two watermills at Bradnocks Marsh to Hannah Neway, with an assignment to William Wright. In 1850 the lessees were named as Hannah Neway and Matthew Johnson. In 1860 William Wright reappears on the scene, named with W. Brittain as the two mill owners.

In December 1893 William Riley, who was in possession of a mill in this area, wrote to the landlords about the scarcity of water and having been compelled to use a steam engine to drive the mill, referring them to the cost of repairs. He wrote again in January 1894, wishing them a Happy New Year, but regretting that he couldn't send them a rent cheque as his bank balance was 'on the wrong side' and that the water wheel was 'going to pieces'. In July 1894 he signed an agreement with the Coventry Church Charities for the lease of Mill Farm and Marsh Farm.

In July 1895 he ordered an oat crusher from A. H. Summers, the millwrights. Three months later in October, he wrote to them, regretting that he could not immediately comply with their request for payment as he had on the previous day bought a flock of sheep, leaving him with an adverse bank balance of £17.

In 1896 correspondence shows that repairs to the mill were being carried out by Messrs Glover & Sons of Warwick, and that he was still waiting for his oat crusher from Summers.

Amazingly, with all his financial problems, Riley continued to work the mill until 1920 when it finally closed down. A few years later the mill was demolished, leaving no clues regarding the type of wheel, nor the number of stones driven. The only remaining features which are still visible are the access road, and a 31 metre long arched brick lined underground culvert, with stone facings, which carried the tail race under the mill. This now runs into an ornamental garden pond and rejoins the river further downstream.

THE WINDMILL

This was built as a stand-by for Bradnocks Marsh water mill, but it appears to have had a very short working life. The mill is not shown on the 1830 O.S. map, but other sources tell us that the mill was in existence in 1806. Shortly after the Birmingham to London railway was built, in 1838, the miller made a claim against the railway company for 'loss of wind' due to the nearby embankment. His claim was unsuccessful, and this may have been the reason for its short life. The mill ceased operating in 1881, and is noted on the 1886 O.S. map as disused. It was converted into a private dwelling in 1940.

HAMPTON WATER MILL

The first recorded reference to a mill in Hampton-in-Arden occurs in the survey carried out in the year 1086, by William I's commissioners for the compilation of the Domesday Book to provide information for tax collection. This water mill would have been sited somewhere on the River Blythe, but its exact location is not known.

In 1276 an inventory was made of the property of William de Arderne, Lord of the Manor of Hampton, which included two water mills. Like most early inventories no maps were ever drawn and no locations given. A later lord, Sir John Peche, who died in 1338 and is buried in the chancel of Hampton Church, signed a quitclaim, relinquishing the site of a water mill, on the River Blythe at Stonebridge. This had previously been leased from the Prior and convent of Kenilworth. In consideration of this the Prior agreed that no corn mill should be built there, but reserved the right to build a 'Fulling' mill, with a millpond at Diddington. This mill, if it had ever been built, would have been used to cleanse, de-grease and thicken the cloth produced from the wool of the convent's sheep.

A royal survey, carried out in December 1649 for Queen Henrietta Maria, widow of Charles I, includes the following paragraph:

All that Cottage or Tenement with a Watergrist Mill now in the tenure or occupation of John Ashurst, the said dwelling house doth conteyne in length XV foote of assize and in breadth XIII foote, and the said mill doth conteyne in length XX foote and in breadth XV foote, with one bay in length XVI foote and the same in breadth. One Cowhouse adjoining the said barne conteyning in length XVI en foote and in breadth VIII. Which said dwelling house, mill and outhouses are all of them covered with thatch abutting upon Meriden Heath on the west and a lane leading to Moldon Bridge on the east and doth contayne in the whole 1 rod and 6 perches.

The mill stood upon the north bank of the river with a short 'leat' – an open watercourse – from the upstream side of the weir to the wheel, which because of the low head of water must have been of the undershot type. Very little of this site, standing on private farmland, can now be seen. Only the base of the weir is visible, and a few sandstone blocks at the foot of the river bank, together with a short length of projecting wall, with possibly 19th Century bricks. A shallow depression, with occasional clumps of marsh grass, runs across the mill field, tracing the line of the old tail race, rejoining the river at a point opposite where the Meriden spillway, now the Horn Brook, discharges. A further leat, presumably a by-pass, still runs from a point about 75 metres upstream to rejoin the river about 200 metres downstream.

HENWOOD WATER MILL

In 1156 Ketelberne de Langdene founded a Benedictine Priory at Estwell, dedicated to Saint Margaret. This priory, by reason of the tall oaks that surrounded it, became known as Henwood, standing near the present Henwood Hall Farm. In 1349 only three of its 15 nuns survived the black death. Alice Waring, of nearby Berry Hall, became the Prioress in 1460 and the priory closed after the Act of Suppression in 1536.

Little is known of the early history of the mill or the millers but it stood unused between 1787 and 1789. In the early 19th century the mill was owned by Mr John Beck of Harbury who also owned the nearby Copt Heath Windmill. In 1804 both mills, occupied by Thomas Marshall, were put up for sale by private treaty. The next known miller was, rather appropriately, called J. T. Miller followed by William Reader until 1884. In 1870 the mill was owned by the pen maker Joseph Gillet. The present mill building appears to date from the late 18th century with some 19th century additions. It is a three storey brick built building, incorporating the mill house, with a tiled roof a weather boarded gable above the mill doors and a timber 'lucam', or hoist cover. When the water wheel was replaced in 1870, it was 4.15 metres in diameter and 3.5 metres wide.

The mill continued to be used until 1934, when it finally closed. It was saved from demolition by Mr W. H. Waller who bought the property and lived in the mill house until 1945. Refurbished by recent owners, the present water wheel retains the shaft, arms and hub casting of the 1870 wheel, but has been fitted with new rims, bearing the words Henwood Mill 1991, James W. Shenton, Founders and J. Fairbanks, Millwright. Most of the mill machinery is still in very good condition.

The mill leat branches off the River Blythe about 450 metres from the mill. When the Birmingham – Warwick Canal, now the Grand Union was built in 1793, two tunnels had to be constructed, one for the river and one for the mill leat, passing through the embankment under the canal. Due to recent changes in the landscape, altering the watercourse, it is unlikely that the mill will ever again be operable.

COPT HEATH WINDMILL

This mill, built in 1792, was brick built with a 4 storey barrel shaped tower. It had four common sails with a wheel and luffing gear in a tail extension of an iron sheeted boat cap. The mill was built as a back-up for Henwood Water Mill. It ceased operating in the 1880s, probably due to the retirement of William Reader, the last miller there in 1884. The sails were removed in 1896 and the tower was demolished in the early 20th century. There is no remaining trace of the mill site, it having vanished under the construction of the M42 embankment and the Old Silhillians sports field.

MERIDEN WATER MILL

There were two corn mills, two houses and a cottage on this site, dating at least from the 1630s, both probably run by the Paddy family. One of these may have been the Hampton Mill, which was only a few hundred metres along the River Blythe, west of the Meriden Mill. The Paddy family continued to operate as millers at various mills in the area. Thomas Paddy, who possibly owned the mill at this time, retired in the 1760s and having no son, he leased it to Joseph Parker, one of another local family of millers. In 1812 Lord Aylesford purchased the mill and land from the Parkers, but the family continued farming and milling for another three generations.

Repairs to the mill, costing £50, were carried out in 1788, and further work was done in the 1830s.

James Henry Parker died in 1913, by which time most of his family had emigrated to Canada, although a Charles Parker is still shown to be in possession of the mill in 1916. In 1939, another family member, 'Harry' Parker, took over of the mill and saved it from being dismantled by a scrap merchant who claimed that he had bought it from a previous owner, and had already started to remove the machinery.

In 1940, due to considerable bomb damage to other working mills, government officials requested the revival of the local Mill. The water supply was much reduced and Mr Parker requested the installation of an engine to drive the mill. The government was not agreeable and so the mill remained idle. The three storey building, mainly brick built with some sandstone walls, is now the office and workshop of the 'Water in the Garden' centre near the end of the Meriden Road.

According to local folklore and ghost stories, in 1876 a man was drowned in the mill pool, which is now silted up and overgrown with trees. He was named as John Male aged 49, from Dudley. His brother attended his funeral in Meriden church.

MERCOTE MILL

The first record of a mill at Mercote is January 19th 1659, when William Hurst, of Berkswell, signed a 21 year agreement leasing three water mills and a windmill in Berkswell from Henry Matthews Esq. of Moorecock Hall. This agreement included provision for fishing in the mill pool and the supply of grain as rent. At the termination of this lease, Henry Matthews signed a similar leasing agreement with Thomas Paddy the elder, a miller from Meriden Heath. This agreement, dated 29th September 1681, covered three parcels of land, Bawdens Meadow, the water mill called Murcutt Mills and the land between the mill and the footbridge, together with the water supply to the mill and various conditions to fishing and floods. The Paddy family remained here as millers until 1760, when Thomas Paddy retired.

It is not known who followed Thomas Paddy, but between 1787 and 1789 the mill stood disused. This may well be the time when the mill, originally noted in Henry Beighton's 1725 survey, was rebuilt, but in 1804 the miller is named as John Phillips who may have continued the occupation until it was recorded as disused, once again, in 1821. Some time later it was converted into a leather mill by Benjamin Smart, then part of it was dismantled with the intention of using it as a silk mill, but there are no records of this activity being pursued. Bankruptcy forced the next owner, John Maice, to sell by auction and there are no further records until 1841 when it was used again for corn milling. It was now owned by eighty year old Elizabeth Britain whose son was a farmer and miller.

Records then show a continual change of ownership until 1925 when the mill became disused once again.

During the Second World war the mill was used to generate electricity for local farm use, and was last used by Mr Harvey in 1943 to *'operate a machine to help Mr Parker of Meriden Mill with a rush of orders'*. What was being produced, or why the rush is not known. The last mill building was brick built, as probably was its predecessors. It was three storeys high with a tiled and gabled roof, with a lucam, or external grain hoist cover, and was built into the 4.3 metre high dam at the west side of its three acre mill pool. The water wheel was enclosed in a separate chamber at the north end of the mill cottage, in an underground conduit, discharging into a small stream beyond it. The tenant in 1944 was Mrs Davis, a retired school teacher. Mr D. Williams, the present tenant of the mill cottage was preceded by Mr G. Pointer. By 1970 when the mill was visited by Tim Booth, the author of Warwickshire Watermills, the mill doors had been removed and the windows were broken. Most of the machinery had been sold for scrap and the water wheel was in such poor condition that it collapsed the following year. For safety reasons, as the mill was close to a public right of way, the building was demolished in about 1994. No trace of it remains except the dam, the dried up mill pool and the underground culvert. The stream from Berkswell Hall lake feeding the millpond ran beneath part of the Mercote Hall stable block in a 60 metre long brick lined tunnel. During the First World War, Mercote Hall was used as a prisoner-of-war camp for German officers. It is rumoured that two of the prisoners escaped through this tunnel. The hall was finally demolished in 1936.

CALDEFORD WATER MILL

The earliest reference to a mill on this site is in a document from the Catalogue of Ancient Deeds, dated 1307. No further reference can be found until a survey of Eastcote Hall, carried out by Thomas Harris on the orders by Robert Smith in 1720. The survey map shows Mill meadow on the north west side of the River Blythe, opposite Barston Lane. This position is later confirmed in surveys of Warwickshire made by Henry Beighton between 1722 and 1725. A more recent survey of the site shows the position of the mill pool, but the original weir can only be seen as a shallow ridge across the river. The banks of the river have been badly eroded by farm traffic crossing the river but no brick, or stonework is exposed. There is a scattering of bricks in the site of the mill pool, but these appear to be nineteenth or twentieth century material. The track of the stream can hardly be seen, but the two pipes where it flowed under Barston Lane are still visible.

About five metres down stream from the weir there are several regular shaped concrete blocks and pieces of concrete, possibly placed here to act as stepping stones. These may date from when the river was diverted during the construction of the M42 motorway.

MILL WHEELS

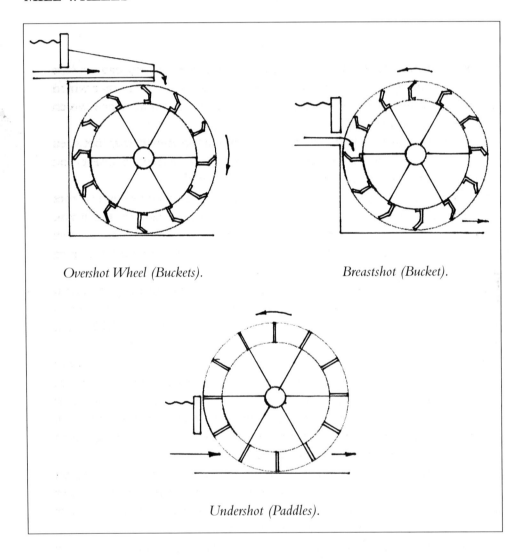

Overshot Wheel (Buckets).

Breastshot (Bucket).

Undershot (Paddles).

CHAPTER FIVE

The Fentham Family and the Trust

There have been several treatise on the subject of George Fentham and his family, among them one researched by Cecil Jordan and another which appears in the Reverend J. C. Adams book 'A Warwickshire Village' which labels him 'A Man of Mystery'.

His beginning and his ending are clearly recorded but the years in between are something of an enigma. To obtain a clearer picture of this man we must look to the earlier generations, and other members of the family.

According to the Reverend Adams, the oldest existing church register names fourteen separate Fentham families, all residing in the Parish of Hampton. Between 1600 and 1700 there are 105 entries in the Hampton Church registers of christenings, marriages and deaths relating to the Fenthams, and 22 entries in the St. Martin's Church registers of the Birmingham Fenthams.

The earliest Fentham recorded in Hampton is Henry, married to Joane, who died in 1623. The inventory of his 'Goods and Chattels' describes his house as a Hall and a Parlour with a chamber over, showing a total worth of £39 5s 10d, and having debts of £22.

Another Henry, not directly related, was the father of George, and eight other children. The oldest, Alice, born 1621, died at the age of 14, Thomas, born 1625, died at the age of ten. Elizabeth, born 1632, died at the age of three. Two other sisters both died before their first birthday, Marie in 1636 and Elizabeth in 1639. Of the nine children, only four survived their father, Anne born in 1622, Henry in 1627, George in 1630 and Dorcas in 1636.

Henry appears to have been one of the more affluent member of Hampton society, a man of the Church, and with Royalist tendencies. He, like other members of the Fentham family, Thomas in 1604, Symon in 1656 and another Thomas in 1661, all held the position of churchwarden.

In his will, dated only two weeks before his death in 1646, he bequeaths *'to my son Henry, one house in Birmingham with all the buildings and appurtenances, this being the rights of ownership, one barn and three closes, called Warners fields lying in Borsley, (this could* possibly be Bordesley, Birmingham). To my other son George a sum of £100, to be reduced to £5 if he inherits my lands in Knowle, and to my daughter Ann my house and lands in Coleshill. To my daughter Dorcas, my cottage in Hampton and the sum of £100'. Although the four named heirs of Henry inherited these properties, the rents paid by the various occupying tenants passed first to his wife Alice until her demise. It is assumed that she was still residing in the Hampton family home.

The law of the day called for a fully evaluated inventory of the house and outbuildings, including all personal items belonging to the deceased. The inventory of Henry's properties and land holdings were valued at £242 0s 10d, being far greater than any other landowner in the village at that time. The family house contained nine rooms on the ground floor and four upper rooms. Most, if not all of the rooms downstairs would have been earth floors, even the Manor House had only two ground floor rooms with boarded floors.

Only two other houses in the village were listed as being larger than Henry Fentham's, the Manor House and the Parson's House, and only nine other properties in Hampton are listed as having more than four rooms. In 1663, however, fifty two homes in Hampton appear in the records for payment of window and hearth tax.

Comfort appeared to be minimal. The hall contained 'one table board, one chair, three stools and three benches. Equipment in the kitchen and buttery comprised three brass pans, four brass pots and four kettles, four brass and two pewter candlesticks and the household plate comprised twelve pewter platters and twelve smaller pieces. Six flitches of bacon and beef hung from the ceiling. The parlour doubled as a bedroom, containing a table board, chest, cupboard and two chairs with a bedstead, a feather bed and a flock bed, two blankets, two bolsters, one pillow, six cushions, a warming pan and the luxury of a rug'.

Distributed amongst the other rooms were four old bedsteads and sundry chests. There were also six spinning wheels, with some yarn and flax, three looms in the buttery, thirteen yards of woollen cloth and a large amount of bed and table linen, all bearing witness to the industry of the female members of the family.

In the barns and outhouses were listed three oxen, seven pigs, eight young beasts, three yearling calves, three weaning calves, twelve sheep and geese and poultry, plus a considerable amount of oats, barley and hay. Even the dung heap in the yard was listed and rated at £1 13s 4d.

The largest single item of value in the inventory was the lease of certain parcels of land worth £70.

It was recorded in the 1649 survey that the Widow Alice Fentham was in the occupation of 56 acres of pasture and meadowland with an annual rent of £27.

And so what of the other members of this Fentham family? It appears that after the death of Henry, his wife, Alice, was financially secure and the four remaining children were well provided for. Alice, always named as the Widow Fentham, re-appears on a number of occasions in Court Baron records of land and property transactions. The eldest daughter Ann is not mentioned again in any Hampton records and so we assume that having reached the age of maturity she moved into the cottage in Coleshill that she inherited from her father, but no records of a possible marriage, or of her burial, can be found in the Coleshill church records.

King Charles I held considerable tracts of land around Hampton, which, after his death in 1649, were confiscated by Cromwell. Henry, George's older brother seems to have followed the edict 'If you cannot beat them, join them' and entered into a contract with Parliamentarian land agents, to purchase a 99 year lease of 173 acres in the parish for a sum of £821 1s 9d. The sub-letting of this land to farming tenants and particularly the sale of timber for shipbuilding would have made young Henry a very wealthy man. Later reports show Henry to be living in a house in Deritend, Birmingham.

In 1649, the Rev. Richard Pretty, vicar of Hampton and a Royalist, was removed from office and re-placed by the Parliamentarian favoured Josiah Packwood. His eldest son, also Josiah, married George's sister, Dorcas, and one wonders, if Henry senior had still been alive whether he would have allowed such a marriage into the enemy camp. Josiah and Dorcus prospered and produced six children, Samuel the oldest, nephew to George became the first official schoolmaster in Hampton. The family of Henry Fentham give the impression of being honest, God fearing people. But there was a darker side to some of the other Fentham's in the parish. Records of the Warwick Sessions in 1640 show that Alice Fentham, wife of Simon, a carpenter, was fined for Riot and Assault.

In 1653, Elizabeth Fentham was whipped for stealing a coat from James Wrightes. In 1679, Ursula Fentham was indicted for being a 'Popish Recusant'. In 1688, Maria Fentham, together with Richard Harding, were indicted for 'Breaking the Assize of Beer' (producing or selling Ale without payment of tax), and in the same year Mary, John and Elizabeth Fentham were fined for 'Encroaching upon the Lords Waste' (Trespassing on the land owned by the Lord of the Manor). The accounts of the Overseer, an official who set the parish rates and was responsible for the well being of the village residents, shows Eustace Fentham as 'a poor man' to be placed into an empty dwelling.

And so to our village benefactor. The actual date of his birth is not known but he was baptised in Hampton Church by the vicar, Simon Grover, on March 30th 1630. Being brought up in such a small community, his early education was quite possibly parent guided at home. With regards to his life in Birmingham, we know that he was apprenticed to a Birmingham mercer, but we do not know at what age, nor for how long. Records of his domestic life are rather confusing. It appears that there were two George Fenthams, both living in Birmingham at this time. Our George makes clear reference in his will to a nephew of 'Bridgett, my late deceased wife', and also to 'Jane my beloved wife', but the records of St. Martin's Church also state, 'wife of George Fentham died 1667', five years before he married Bridgett. Was this a third wife or the wife of the other George?

Birmingham at this time was no more than a line of smithies, workshops and houses from the hamlet of Deritend to a small cluster of streets around St. Martin's Church. The country, during George's early years, was in turmoil. In 1643, when George was thirteen, Prince Rupert led a royalist attack upon the foundries and blade factories in Deritend, and destroyed 80 properties. With the Royalist forces based in Aston Hall and Cromwell's in Edgbaston Hall, there were continual skirmishes in areas around Birmingham. Captured Royalists were isolated by being sent to Coventry jail, hence the origin of the phrase 'Sent to Coventry'.

In 1649, when George was nineteen, Charles I was executed and by the time he reached the age of twenty three the country was under the control of the Protector of the Commonwealth of England.

Is it possible that George, like others before, and most certainly those after him, built his business and made his fortunes from the great demands of a country at war.

In 1676, at the age of 46, we see the first official record of George's activities, in Birmingham, none of which bears any relationship to the business of a mercer or draper. He is shown to be the tenant of the largest area of land owned by the Governors of King Edward VI School. This was originally sited at the bottom of New Street, eventually moved in 1930 and rebuilt in Harborne, and replaced with The Odeon Cinema. A hand drawn sketch, found in the Birmingham Records Office, shows this large area of farmland, leased to George for the sum of £74 10s a year, stretching from the top of New Street to the present-day area of Ladywood. A second, commercial area of tenements and small businesses, situated around the Bull Ring and Digbeth, on school land, was also owned by George. It was this area, around Moor Street, that Henry, his elder brother lived, and the widowed Jane Fentham took up residence after his death.

In 1683, he is noted as one of seven Birmingham residents who paid for a new roof on the Market Cross, and in 1687 he leased a 'Croft' in Moor Street for 89 years at 32s per year, to dig for clay to make bricks. A year later he gave £15 worth of bricks for the building of a Roman Catholic Chapel and Priest's House

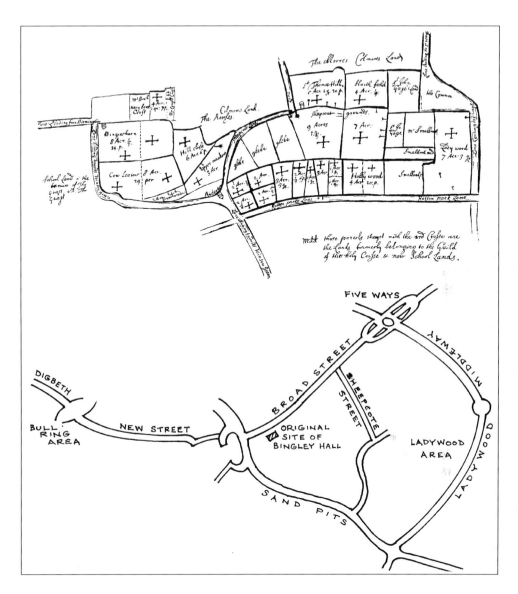

Top - Copy of a hand drawn map found in Birmingham Reference library, dated 1675, showing the land owned by the Governors of the King Edward VI School, and leased to George Fentham. The 'Lane leading to Birmingham' would eventually become New Street running into the old Birmingham Market area of the Bull Ring and Digbeth.

Bottom - The second, simplified present day map shows the area of land between Broad Street, Sand Pits and the Ladywood Middleway. Its is thought that Bingley Hall was named and built upon the old Binglierbarn field.

in Masshouse Lane. Is this evidence of a liberal religious attitude? The chapel was consecrated in August 1688 and demolished three months later by the 'Birmingham Rabble', a group of anti-catholic militants. It appears that George, the apprenticed mercer and draper, made most of his fortune from other forms of business and the sub-letting of land and properties.

The next recorded event is the publication of his will, following his death in 1698.

A vast seventeen page document was left in the trust of four executors, two Birmingham businessmen and two Hampton landowners, George Bradnocks, possibly the owner of the present Bradnocks Marsh and Robert Loggins, son of the steward to the Lord of the Manor.

He leaves sums of money to a number of named beneficiaries, £5 to each of the Executors, £100 to his personal servant, £10 each to the household servants and varying amounts to fourteen relatives of his, and of his first wife, a grand total of £1,100. In addition he set up accounts, which were sufficient to cover four annuities. £40 to his widow Jane, £2 to Elizabeth Hunt, a former servant, and to the two areas that had been important to him in his lifetime.

To Hampton there was an annuity of £30, of which £20 was to be paid half yearly 'to such person appointed to teach school but', and here he looks to his own family, 'my Will is that Samuel Packwood, my nephew, who teaches school there shall have the £20 for as long as he continues to teach'. As it happened, Samuel died in 1720 and never received his inheritance. The other £10 was split equally and distributed half to the ten poorest families and half for the placement of sons of the poorest inhabitants into an apprenticeship.

Birmingham received £20, half given like Hampton to a person selected by the inhabitants living within two hundred yards of the Bull Ring, to teach both male and female, their letters, to spell and read English. Two strange anomalies here; in Hampton he specifies the teaching of boys only, but both boys and girls in Birmingham. Also he specifies 'English' when most schooling at this time was still conducted in Latin. The remaining £10 was to provide, 'such poor women, of whom ten are to be widows, living within this same area of the Bull Ring with coats'. Later reports show that between ten and twenty shawls, gowns and bonnets were distributed each year to these selected, poor women.

In 1724, a Blue Coat School was built in the corner of St. Phillip's churchyard on what is now Colmore Row. By 1741, it was agreed to accept children from the Fentham Charity, at a rate of £4 5s per year.

These children were clothed in a uniform, which was dark green in colour, rather than the standard dark blue worn by the other pupils.

Before any of this could be activated however, a problem arose that was to cause a delay of forty years. A complaint was filed in the Court of Chancery against the trustees and executors of the Will and by the time this had been resolved all those responsible had passed away. By 1731 two of the heirs of the original trustees were in financial trouble and several tenants of George Fentham land were in arrears with their rents. The whole affair was in complete turmoil and so in December 1737 the Court of Chancery ordered new trustees to be appointed and by the following year, now forty years after his death, the charity was re-established. The trust estate was divided equally, giving Hampton income from properties and land in Handsworth, Smethwick and Oldbury, and to Birmingham, Erdington, Aston and Handsworth.

Over the years there have been noticeable changes to the original application of the charity. Government Acts which established national funding for education and general welfare caused the Charity Commissioners to carry out an appraisal, and in 1906 they introduced a new charity scheme.

The Hampton and Birmingham schemes are broadly similar in their statements. Both cover the general benefits of the poor, with funding to hospitals, convalescent homes and nursing care, and they both fund an educational foundation, but Hampton goes much further. In 1906, Birmingham provided £10 each year to be applied for educational purposes, but not related to any particular school.

Hampton gave an annual sum of £500 to the 'George Fentham Educational Foundation' for the care and maintenance of the Boys' and Girls' Schools and the house and garden of the Schoolmaster and Schoolmistress. The remainder provided for a cottage hospital with two beds, said to be somewhere in Meriden Road, with a salaried resident nurse, a recreational ground to be accessible to the inhabitants, a reading room, library or working men's club and the support of any museum or exhibition. In addition to all this, selected poor pensioners were to be paid a weekly stipend.

To this present day, the Trust, as it is now known, still funds the educational requirements of the school and children in the village, still provides financial assistance for the poorer residents and makes funds available to the Hampton History Group and its displays in the Heritage Centre.

CHAPTER SIX

Hampton Schools

HAMPTON-IN-ARDEN SCHOOLS

In the early eighteen hundreds there was an increasing concern for the high level of ignorance, particularly amongst the poorer groups of society, and the appalling conditions of young children working in the mills and factories. Religious bodies, advocating a more formal, full time style of education for all children was, at first, met with much opposition from the factory owners, enjoying cheap labour, and from parents of large families reaping greater financial benefits.

In 1833 the first State Grant for school building was introduced, followed in 1846 with grant aid towards the salaries of teaching staff. The greatest landmark in education, however, was the Education Act of 1870, which demanded that children, between the ages of five and thirteen, should attend regular, full time education.

Some schools did exist before this period, run privately by dedicated caring people in their own homes, some funded by the Church and some, like the Hampton School, by charitable organisations. George Fentham, in his will dated 1690, bequeathed thirty pounds, twenty pounds of which was to be paid – 'to such Person as shall be appointed to and lawfully teach school in Hampton to male children of the inhabitants of the Parish and especially of the Poorer sort'.

A codicil of this will, dated 1697, nominates George Fentham's nephew, Samuel Packwood as an executor and describing him as the Hampton-in-Arden schoolmaster. We can assume from this that the education of some village children was in progress, possibly as early as 1690. There is one other vague recorded statement that – 'with the assistance of two other people, not named, provision was made for two charity schools in the village, one for boys and one for girls'. The Tithe Map of 1841 shows the early Boys School on the corner of Fentham Road and Butcher Road, and a School Room, in a cottage on the High Street, just below the Church. It would be reasonable to assume that this was an early school for the education of girls.

It was not until 1782, almost one hundred years after the educational bequest, that the first official school was built in Hampton. The Trustees of the George Fentham Estate paid one hundred and fifty two pounds three shillings eight pence

The new Boys' School opposite the old school building in Fentham Road. The present George Fentham Endowed School has been created by a number of extensions to this building.

and one farthing for the construction of a house for the schoolmaster to live and teach in. That house, now known as Fentham Cottage, carries a plaque dedicated to the George Fentham School and the responsible Trustees.

After Samuel Packwood, the first schoolmaster, there are no records to be found of any succeeding teachers until John Tibbitts, resident schoolmaster, in around 1795. In 1812, possibly due to an increase in pupil attendance, an extension was built to the cottage, to be used as a schoolroom, now of course the village library. This was to remain the village school for boys until 1914 when the new school building was erected on the opposite side of Fentham Road.

In these early years, between the mid and late nineteenth century, the two schools were closely connected with the church, but were never 'Church Schools'. The Hampton vicars were either Chairmen, or one of the School Managers and paid regular weekly visits to the schools, sometimes social, but mostly in a professional capacity to check on attendance registers and the level of education. In 1875 the school logbook reports visits by Rev. T. J. Morris to take lessons in Reading, Religious Instruction and Arithmetic. His reports were passed onto the school managers for inspection and would certainly to have kept the Headmaster and Teachers well on their toes.

Education was very basic, the three R's were the backbone of the system, together with Religious Instruction and Singing. A song list was established, learnt each year, and then examined at an annual inspection.

By the late eighteen hundreds both of the schools had two annual visits from inspectors, a Diocesan Inspection and a Government Inspection, both of which took the form of an examination.

A Diocesan examination held on July 2nd 1886 reported that 36 children were presented and examined in – Catechism, O.T. Bible, N.T. Bible, Christian Year and Prayer Book.

The Government examination covered the wider aspect of education, but it is interesting to note that the two inspections were both led, by a Churchman. The church maintained its close connection with the schools, overseeing the standards of teaching and learning, later to be carried out by a body of H.M. Inspectors established by the Government.

The weekly timetable and the timing of school holidays were very much more flexible than today.

An entry in the Hampton School log book states – 'The Summer holidays in 1875 were fixed, by the Managers, to be from August 3rd to August 27th, and conditionally upon the harvest from September 21st for a further two weeks. In the October of this year a number of boys were excused, or just did not turn up during the period of potato harvesting. This habit of family business before education continued right up to the second world war when children of farming parents were permitted 'time off' to help during these busy times of the farming calendar.

Some of the reasons quoted in the log book show the agricultural influence in the village.

In August 1875 – 76 boys were given permission to be absent from school on half days to 'scare birds' from the corn, and in September a number of children of farming families were given permission to help with the harvest.

Each year in the late eighteen hundreds the girls were given the day free 'after morning prayers' to collect wild flowers to decorate the village Flower Show Marquee.

On January 19th 1875 both schools were closed for a 'Half Day Treat'. They were invited by the Rev. Morris to celebrate his wife's birthday. There were times when the schools were closed for other reasons – being used as an examination centre, or to distribute clothing to the poor by the Clothing Club. Half day holidays were always given on certain important dates in the calendar – Ascension Day, Shrove Tuesday and Empire Day.

Church services were held but the children were not obliged to attend. The Parish magazine provides a detailed report of a 'School Trip to London', which took place on September 13th 1886. A sufficient sum of money was collected by Miss Houghton and Mr Hope to enable them to take a party of 40 boys and girls to visit London. By the day of the trip this number had increased to 60, guided by 11 teachers and parents. By train, then by omnibus they visited the Zoological Gardens and had a conducted tour of the Houses of Parliament and Westminster Abbey.

This was followed with a steamboat trip on the Thames followed by refreshments in a 'Cocoa House' and a visit to the exhibition of the Underground Railway. They departed from London at 12.10am and arrived back in Hampton at 3.40am and were then served with tea in the Girls School.

This must have been exhausting for all concerned, but the governors did allow a holiday on that next day.

Apart from this, 1886 was a rather tragic year. March produced such heavy snow that only 8 children attended school, and torrential rain in May caused very little attendance. Later in the year an epidemic of measles across the village caused the school to close for one week in October and three weeks in November.

Even the Headmaster had his share of the problems. In this same year four boys were reported to the head for passing 'grossly indecent papers' to the girls. Thomas Hope, the Headmaster, administered a 'sound thrashing' to the boys with a birch rod. The parents of one boy consulted a solicitor with the intention of seeking justice for the injury to their son. The school managers offered to pay any legal costs on behalf of the Headmaster but the boy was expelled for other misdemeanours and the issue was closed. Signs of poverty and poor living conditions were also very apparent. In 1896 the school log book reported that a boy was taken to the clinic *"having severe skin infection and head lice causing hair loss"*, and another boy was sent home, *"as his clothes required mending so badly that his appearance was indecent"*.

In October 1903 the Leamington Gazette reported the disappearance of a schoolmaster stating, *"After eleven days the disappearance of Mr Thomas Hope is still a mystery. Headmaster of the school, an active member of the village, he had been elected earlier in the year as National Grand Master of the Order of Oddfellows. He leaves a wife and ten children"*. There were later reports that he had absconded to Canada, but this was never confirmed.

Only one record can be found of the early education of the girls in Hampton. In December 1848 the rent for the Schoolroom was set at 1/- per week and in the same month James Osborne received £2 for the repair of the chimney in the girls schoolroom. The mistress, Miss Wilday, received £15 as her half years salary,

The Girls and Infants' School building photographed in the early 1900s. The school mistresses house attached to the school can just be seen on the left.

and the Infant School mistress, Sara Miles, received £4. The attendance varied between fifteen and forty, 'according to the time of year'.

In 1849 the Bishop of Worcester laid the foundation stone for the first formal school for girls. By 1850, at a cost of one thousand three hundred pounds, to the George Fentham Trust, a teachers house and a school was opened on the site off the High Street in what was later to become Wellmeadow Grove. This was divided into three teaching areas, two for girls between the ages of seven and fourteen and one for mixed infants. No expense appears to have been spared with the opening ceremony. The final cost of £15 was as much as the half year's salary paid to the schoolmistress. Little is known of the first few years of this school but it is reasonable to assume that Miss Wilday and Sara Miles continued as mistresses in charge. Later records show that in 1854 Miss Mary Ann Pratt was the mistress and Joseph Smith was the master of the George Fentham Charity Schools in Hampton. From early in 1871 regular reports, of the educational and social activities of the Girls' School, began to appear in the Village Chronicle. The Government and Diocesan inspections continually praised both teachers and the pupils. In June 1874 Mr Edward Houghton, the Diocesan Inspector, gave high praise to the Schoolmistress, Mrs Houghton and the Pupil Teacher, Miss

Houghton – coincidence? More interesting is the large amount of village social activity that occurred here. We must remember that at this time, before the existence of Fentham Hall and the Church Hall, the only community rooms were attached to the village Inns, and so a fairly sizeable schoolroom was an obvious choice for social gatherings and meetings. During much of its lifetime, the building was used, at least once each month, for lectures and magic lantern shows, the first by Sir Frederick Peel on 'The Story of Greek History'. Mostly the events were Musical Evenings, Piano Recitals, Glee Singers and amateur singing competitions. plays,

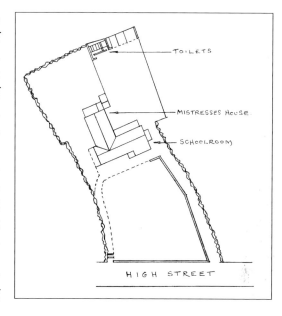

A plan of the Girls and Infants School leading off the High Street, now Wellmeadow Grove.

playlets and farces given by Drama groups from many parts of the Midlands, school pantomimes, recitations and readings, many from village residents.

As this became more and more popular, it was necessary to book seats, named and priced as, 'Front Seats' 1/- and 'Rear Seats' 6d. Profits from these events were sent to selected charities and later for the village Church Organ Fund.

The Girls' school remained active, on this site, until 1940 when it was decided to enlarge the new Boys' School, built in 1914, to house all children of school age in the village. The old school for girls was commandeered, for the duration of the war, by the Home Guard and then for over twenty years it became the home of the Women's Institute before being demolished to make way for six bungalows for the elderly.

1914 had brought about great changes to education in Hampton. The boys moved from the premises that had been their home since 1782 to the new school building on the opposite side of Fentham Road, with the added luxury of playing fields and an area for school gardens. Two months later came the start of World War I and those gardens were to be put to great educational and practical use. By March of 1915 twelve plots were prepared, a tap was fitted for outside watering, and boot scrapers were installed.

47

A gardening class in the Boys' School, possibly taken around the time of the First World War.

A variety of practical lessons evolved from these school gardens. Notebooks and diaries were kept containing details of progress reports, summaries of crops, weights and value – Practical Arithmetic – Profit and Loss accounts. Drawing - plans of planting areas. Nature Study, the Chemistry of Gardening, and planting practices.

Meteorological observations were taken recording rainfall and temperature. This project was obviously rated very highly. In July 1917, Mr Webb, a visiting inspector, passed plans, photographs and a detailed survey of the gardens to a committee of the Board of Agriculture.

All the lessons in gardening and woodwork were taken by Mr Frodin, the headmaster and whenever possible the articles for use in the garden were made, by the boys, in the woodwork room.

In 1917 the log book reports that 2cwt 7stones 12lbs of potatoes and quantities of vegetables, parsley and thyme were delivered to the Red Cross 'Voluntary Aid Detachment' military hospital in Fentham Hall. In this year the boys also collected 15 shillings towards a bed for wounded soldiers at this local hospital, which was named 'The Childrens Bed'.

A group photograph of the girls and infants, possibly in the 1930s.

Schools across the country were 'doing their bit' towards the war effort. In September 1917 the boys from Fentham School were given time off to pick horse chestnuts to be sent to a synthetic products plant in Kings Lynn for the processing of acetone used in high explosives. In this one month the quantity collected was nearly one ton. Over four days in late September and early October 1918, the boys were given half, or full day holidays, from school to pick blackberries – 'For the Government'.

No reason is given for this government involvement and so we could possibly assume that this was a national jam – making campaign.

In 1924, the garden activities were further expanded by the delivery of a Beehive, four frames of Bees and bee keeping appliances from Miss Johnson in Dorking, Surrey.

In 1933 the Warwickshire Education Authority considered amalgamating the Boys, Girls and Infants Schools. By 1934, the conversion plans had been drawn up and in 1939 Mr Tulet became the new headmaster. In September of 1940, the old girls school had been closed, the Boys School had now been extended and for the first time all village schoolchildren, between the ages of five and eleven, were being taught in one building. The children then passed on to senior education, either at the newly built Lode Heath School in Solihull, to Solihull Grammar School, if they passed the entrance examination, or to Coventry Technical School.

At the start of the Second World War the managers refused to allow the school to open until adequate Air Raid Shelters had been dug across the school playing fields for the boys.

When the school reopened, provision was made for thirty of the girls to be sheltered in the cellars of The Manor, another twenty five at the Vicarage and twenty five at The Engine. The first day was given to Gas Mask drill, taking cover and other precautions. The school day was reduced to four hours (9am - 1pm).

The wooden hut, originally used as the woodwork room in the First World War and then converted into a room for use as the 'Old Boy's Club', was requisitioned as billets for eighteen men of the local Ack-Ack Battery. By 1942 this served as a Club Recreation and Refreshments Room used in the evenings by members of H. M. Forces. A kitchen was installed, for use as a School Canteen, and on the opening day fifty dinners were cooked and served at 4d per head. The opening of the new school brought about other changes to the educational system. There was an introduction of 'School Broadcasting' an activity that was never defined, and a very elementary form of school transport was started. In 1940, there was natural panic everywhere, the school timetable was continually disrupted by Air Raid warnings and through November and December of that year 255 school hours had been spent in shelters. At the beginning of 1941, however, general concern for safety diminished and the Managers, with the consent of the parents, decided that schoolwork should continue unless immediate danger threatened. It was only after continual bombing of the Coventry area, in May 1941, that two Stirrup Pumps were supplied to the school. From now on the only disruption to normal school life was when children were given time off to help with the war effort in collecting waste products for salvage, picking fruit and twisting peoples arms for money.

In March 1941, 'War Weapons Week' the school collected £1,021 on the first day and £1,600 by the end of the week. By May of this year the total amount collected since the beginning of the war was £4,000. In March 1942, the collection for 'Warships Week' amounted to £15,157 and in May 1943 a School Group collected £4,594 for 'Wings for Victory Week'. By September the schools total collection reached £20,000. A further £7,936 was added to this for 'Salute the Soldier Week' in May 1944 and 2,200 'Ship Halfpennies' were collected for 'Merchant Navy Comforts Week' Considering the small number of people in the village at this time, and that the earnings of some were not that high, this is a staggering amount of money collected by one school.

The children were co-opted to collect salvage and books from round the village and in two weeks came up with 6,500 books and a ton of salvage. David Topley was the champion collector with a personal total of 900 books.

A group photograph of the boys outside the old school, now the village library. The young girl in the front row is the daughter of the Head Teacher, Mr W. A. Frodin, shown with his wife who was an assistant teacher in the school.

From the school gardens came a regular supply of fresh fruit and vegetables, much of which was donated to the local hospital. In September 1943 a selection of vegetables was sent to Solihull Horticultural Show and won Third Prize. The children were given time off school to pick fruit from the hedgerows and on one occasion, 42 pounds of jam was made in the school kitchen.

Possibly the most important change to the future of the school was the formation of the first Parents Association. In July 1943 at a meeting of forty parents, teachers and managers, chaired by the headmaster, Mr Tulet, the Fentham Junior School Parents Association was formed, with an annual subscription of 2/6d. For the first time this brought a closer co-operation between parents and teaching staff. Early minutes of meetings show a greater involvement between the parents and the school with the planning of the first Nursery Class and discussions involving school transport to the senior schools. But the main purpose of the P.T.A. has always been on a more social level, raising funds for the benefit of the school.

The war ended in May 1945 and by the end of the summer holidays all 'Baffle Walls' and window protection had been removed. There are no reports of any celebrations in the school but the children decorated the main gates with Flags and Shields of the Allied Nations, all made in the school.

Easter 1963 brought the closure of Bickenhill School and the pupils were brought by school transport to Hampton. Fentham School was extended and reorganised into five classes, with new staff to accommodate the new intake. In 1967, two more classrooms were added and in 1976 further changes occurred with the addition of a new Head Teacher's office and a library.

The main school building now houses seven classrooms, a hall used for morning assembly, P.E. and as a dining room, and a resources room for science and technology. A separate building has since been added, as a Nursery Unit with its own 'teacher in charge' and a nursery nurse.

Over the years the Village Chronicle has provided information of a number of other educational establishments and activities.

The Rev. T. J. Morris, vicar of Hampton from 1866 to 1906 ran a small school for girls, with the help of a governess, to be educated alongside his daughters. In 1904, Miss Florence Austin, originally a governess to a Hampton family, opened Ardenvale School for Girls in Diddington Lane, which was advertised regularly, in the chronicle, until 1924. She is remembered by some of the older residents of the village as a Children's Hour B.B.C. Aunt.

From 1927 to 1939 the Chronicle contained advertisements from four separate tutors. They included Mrs Morgan based at a house called Laxey and Mrs Redfern at Dei Gratia, who both offered private tuition and coaching for examinations for 'Girls and Small Boys'. Mr Weddon-Burgess of Rhosymedre, a professor of music, who gave tuition in organ and pianoforte and Mrs Howe of Hubenon offered Private Piano lessons. These tutors did not appear to have any professional connection, but it was strange to see that all four houses were in Eastcote Lane.

CHAPTER SEVEN

The Railway

The country's canal system had served the growing industrial areas of the Midlands and the North of England for a number of years but this slow, ponderous form of transport was unable to cope with the fast growing volume of business and trade. The linking of northern industry to London, through the expanding midland cities, with a faster form of transport became essential, and what better than the new form of locomotion. Routes of railway tracks were being planned across the country and obviously the planners had chosen the line of least geographical resistance with the cheapest financial outlay. It just so happened that a tiny rural Warwickshire village, called Hampton-in-Arden, lay exactly in the centre of all this activity, which would, over the years, greatly affect the physical and social structure of the village. Not only did Hampton lie on the main route from Liverpool to London, but was also to accommodate a junction with another branch line to Derby.

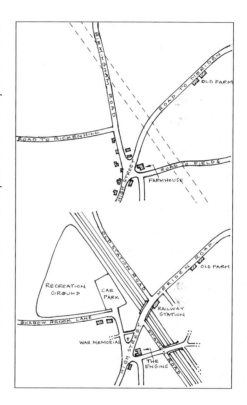

Two maps of the area at the bottom of the High Street before and after the construction of the railways line, showing the changes made to the roads.

The earliest thoughts of a rail network date back to 1808, when William James, a surveyor from Henley-in-Arden proposed the formation of a 'General Railroad Company' with a main line between Birmingham and London. It

The Railway Station as it was first built in 1884. The main building is on the left above the covered walkway up to road level. Note the chimneys on the waiting rooms.

was not until 1823 however that the London & Birmingham Railway Company as it became known, was formed.

There had been a great amount of dissension by the nobility, fearing the physical disturbance to their estates, and only after the allocation of money for land purchase was increased from £250,000 to £750,000 did the Lords agree. The final route plan was adopted in September 1830, the Royal Assent was then given in 1833, and George Stephenson and his son Robert were appointed as joint engineers. Within a few months, George was attached to another railway project and Robert was left in sole charge. The excavation of the cutting through the centre of the village was carried out in an unusual way. Normally cuttings were trenched out and the spoil removed sideways, but Robert Stephenson decided to trench from each end and pull the soil outwards to build the two adjacent embankments., one towards Marston Green and the other, to the south, towards Berkswell. This whole section of line, between Rugby and Birmingham, was opened for passengers in April 1838, and for goods traffic in September of that year. The first train, consisting of four first and five, second class carriages, took fifty minutes to travel the eighteen miles between Birmingham to Coventry. All carriages were open

A goods train joining the main line after leaving the goods yard at the bend in Marsh Lane.

sided and only the first class had a roof. The mail trains were the fastest, travelling from Birmingham to London in five hours, and the passenger service, stopping at all stations, taking eight hours. The cost of a first class, one - way only fare was thirty shillings (£1.50) and second-class twenty shillings (£1). During the first four weeks the London & Birmingham Railway Company carried 50,238 passengers, who purchased tickets worth £35,428. This enormous amount of money was obviously brought about by the novelty of the new form of transport. By the end of the first year the takings were considerably reduced.

It was the proposed route from Derby that caused great problems. Two many powerful and influential men with conflicting ideas almost brought about the cancellation of this project. The proprietors of this Birmingham and Derby Junction Railway, headed by Sir Oswald Mosley, included a number of eminent Birmingham businessmen and Midland landed gentry, one of whom was Sir Robert Peel, Member of Parliament for Tamworth and later to become Prime Minister. Between them they raised £630,000 in £100 share lots. The original plans for the final section of the line from Coleshill by-passed Hampton, crossing the Birmingham to Coventry road at Stonebridge and joining the main London line near to the Hampton packhorse bridge, and

A train on the Stonebridge Railway crossing the railway bridge over Old Station Road. The turn into The Grove can just be seen under the bridge. Both the line and the bridge have long since been demolished.

was known as The Stonebridge Railway. At some point the Earl of Aylesford made a request to Parliament to consider a route further away from his estate at Packington Park, and as the Earl had offered to pay for the amendment to the Act, it was agreed. In 1838 the line was re-routed through Hampton.

In the early years, the signalling and control of train movement was carried out by a railway police force, kitted out in green uniforms with top hats. They were stationed along the track at regular intervals, using green flags in the daytime and lamps at night. A method of semaphore was devised adapted from the system used by the navy and was later replaced by the signal box.

Hampton Station then sat at the junction of two important lines, and was considered to be something of a showpiece. For the first ten years Hampton station was known as Derby Junction, then changed to Hampton Junction and then in 1872 became plain Hampton. In 1884, a new station was built, under the control of the London & North Western Railway, in what we now know as the junction of High Street and Meriden Road. This was named Hampton-

The old station in Old Station Road showing the island platform between the main London line and the Stonebridge.

in-Arden Station and was used specifically for passenger travel. Queen Victoria, and a large royal party, graced the station with her presence when travelling on to Drayton Manor, to visit Sir Robert Peel.

The old Hampton Station, still run by the Midland Railway, was now used mainly for goods traffic. Because of the re-positioning of the station the High Street, from the church down to the station, became known as Station Road.

This original station building was unusual in its design, looking a little like the early turnpike toll houses, and was listed as 'first class'. The station house, occupied by the stationmaster, was a three-roomed single storey building, with a small separate ticket and parcels office. In 1842, the Justices granted a licence to sell alcoholic drinks in the station house, and for twenty-three years Hampton Station had its own licensed bar run by the owner of The Engine Hotel. Two large engine sheds were built, with their own sidings, to house and maintain four locomotives. The station layout consisted of three platforms. One was attached to the front of the station house, and an island platform, which separated the two sets of lines. The third platform built on the far side was used for the main line London to Birmingham traffic. A twice-daily inter-city service had been established and over the years was well used by local

The Railway Station and bridge showing a very narrow road across the bridge.

residents. In May 1980 the service was transferred from Hampton to Birmingham International Station, providing a service for the Airport and the National Exhibition Centre.

There are no records of any specific use of this railway during the First World War. In 1917 all passenger services on the Derby line ceased but the goods traffic increased with the coming of Wyckham Blackwell and his new sawmill. Trees were transported to Hampton to be converted into timber planking for the construction of railway wagons, and the resulting sawdust was then taken to Hams Hall power station. There are records of an agreement, made in March 1927, between the London Midland & Scottish Railway Company and Arthur Henry Blackwell, then a Hampton coal & coke merchant. For the sum of £1 per year, he had the privilege of right of entry down the railway company's private road, now Station Road, through a pair of gates, erected and maintained by him, for the purpose of taking cattle and farm vehicles onto his land.

During the Second World War, sand, taken from a quarry in Packington, was loaded onto trains at Hampton Junction and taken to new wartime airfields for the construction of runways. An engine towing an open truck, mounted with a mobile gun travelled daily up and down the line from Hampton. Whether it actually fired on anything is not known. There are reports of a secret Air Ministry control centre based at Hampton, and also a factory making hand grenades. It is possible that time has distorted some memories and that these were one and the same.

Goods services had ended in 1930 and the Maxtoke to Hampton section remained unused until 1951 when the line was officially closed and the track removed. At about this time the old station house was converted into a private residence. In the two years 1963-1964, the Hampton sidings were lifted, the bridge across Old Station Road was demolished, and by 1965 the old Hampton junction had ceased to exist.

CHAPTER EIGHT

Village Inns

There were at one time seven licensed premises with the village. This number has been reduced to the present three by three of the premises closing and one, the Malt Shovel, is now outside the village due to boundary changes.

The first mention of a licensee who can be traced to a particular pub in Hampton was Henry Gilbert in 1779 who was the licensee at the Ring of Bells. This is one of the pubs that is no longer a public house and the building is now known as "The Old Ring of Bells". He was the first of four generations of Gilberts who between them held the licence for nearly 100 years. But the family lived in the village long before this date. There was a Thomas Gilbert who was a churchwarden in 1709 and the name occurs in the parish registers of the 1600s.

Henry was the first of four generations at the Ring of Bells. At the age of 27 (in 1773) he married Elizabeth Fyfield by licence at the parish church. They were to have five children, the eldest of which was named William who was born in 1775. In turn William married and had children of his own, one of whom was to take his grandfather's place behind the bar of the Ring of Bells. But before this took place Henry's widow became the "landlord" continuing for a further four years before handing over to her grandson, John.

John Gilbert also married an Elizabeth, maybe a close relative as her surname was Gilbert as well. They were both in their early twenties when they became "mine hosts" at the Ring of Bells and before long, in the 1841 tithe return they were listed as owner/occupiers. The entry says that there was two roods and twenty perches of land that went with the pub which would have extended as far as the public footpath now situated to the south of Belle Vue Terrace. The pub had several low ceilinged rooms including the brewhouse where the beer would have been brewed. In the early days, before the invention of the hand pulled pump, the beer would have been served to customers from jugs.

Of John and Elizabeth's eight children, five boys and three girls, three were to be involved in the pub. John senior, when making his will expressed the wish that

The Ring of Bells showing Eboralls the butcher next door. Date unknown.

his wife would have an interest in the property and business for her lifetime and upon her death this would pass to their second son John. Henry the first born had died in infancy. John junior inherited the pub on his mother's death in 1870. John senior had a carpentry business that he ran as a sideline and this was left to the other two surviving sons. John's sisters were promoted from barmaids to victuallers on their mother's death. It appears that John junior and his brother William ran the carpentry business and there is a record of the brothers being paid £2 12s for the erection of a pew in the church. Both brothers were successful as the land return of 1873 shows William owning over 12 acres of land and John nearly seven acres. Seven of the Gilbert family are recorded as buried in the churchyard.

Several licensees were to follow although the Gilberts remained the freeholders until 1878. One of these was James Wall (or Tall), a former butler to the Peel family, and he opened a large tea room at the rear of the pub. In January 1902 he gave a grand concert in this room. James remained at the Ring of Bells until his death in 1908 aged 50.

The final night at the Ring of Bells in 1938.

Further licensees were to follow including Henry Mitchell before it became part of the Mitchells and Butler's group in 1922. The last licensees were Mr and Mrs H. W. Jones who held a farewell supper and dance before the Ring of Bells closed at 10pm on 11th October 1938 when the licence was transferred to the Greville Arms in Solihull.

One of the pubs not included in our list of licensed premises is the Red Lion. The Rev. Adams refers to the fact that one of the original pews in the church belonged to the Red Lion. John Gee is listed in the licences from 1793 to 1820 but receives no further mention. It is believed that the building more recently known as West End cottage was the Red Lion. The mystery is compounded because in 1861 the census enumerator starts by saying that he started by the house lately know by the sign of the "Yeoman" when he is clearly starting from the house in Solihull Road nearest to Knowle Road.

The White Lion first appears in the list of Warwickshire licences in 1801 although the building is much older and was probably a farmhouse. A deed of 1835 refers to it as *"heretofore called by the name of the Crown late of the Dog Inn and now called or known by the name of the White Lion"*. It was referred to in the list of licences as the White Lion from 1801 until 1828 when the licensee is given as William Smith. A gap then appears although William Smith is listed as living at the White Lion in the voters list of 1833.

The White Lion, date unknown, showing Eboralls the butcher next to the pub and yet another shop next to the present Post Office.

The next person shown as the landlord is George Jennings in the 1841 census. He had a wife Hannah and four children. He was not the owner as in the tithe apportionment of 1841 a William Bint is the owner with George as the tenant. In directories of this period George is also given as being a butcher so we imagine that he had enough land to graze cows for his butchery business. As we have seen in other pubs it was not unusual for landlords to have a second occupation.

Further tenancies occur over the years some only staying for short periods – ten years seems to be the average. An advertisement shortly before the end of the nineteenth century says that the White Lion was a commercial inn providing wine, spirits and cigars. And that they also provided picnics for small parties at a moderate charge and that they had first class stabling accommodation. By the early years of the twentieth century it was advertising to cyclists saying that large and small parties are catered for and describing itself as the ancient hostelry with modern facilities.

A tale concerning the White Lion occurred in the mid-1960s when a rather portly gentleman walked in through the rear door of the pub before the entrance hall and toilets had been constructed. He was crossing the room towards the bar counter and the floor collapsed under him. The only thing that saved him falling right through to the floor of the cellar was the rug which wrapped itself around

The Engine in the 1950s.

him. The rear area of the side bar was closed for some weeks while the old floor boarding and joists were replaced. When the floor boarding was completely removed lines of grain could be seen along the joists. Pat Long, the publican of the White Lion, collected a small amount of this grain and took it to the horticultural research establishment at Wellesbourne. Tests were carried out in the laboratory and they came to the conclusion that it was a type of brewing grain used to brew ale in the seventeen and eighteen hundreds. The rear area of the side bar had obviously been a grain store at some time and possibly the front area was the brewing room.

The Engine as its name suggests has links with the railway. In fact it was originally known as the Railway and was opened in 1838, the same year in which the Birmingham to London Railway was opened. In the first planned layout for the Birmingham and London Railway, produced in 1835, the building now known as the Engine was shown as a farmhouse with outbuildings, garden and orchard now owned by John Harris and occupied by David Marks. We believe that it was then bought by the railway company and used as offices by the supervisor and then turned into the Railway Hotel. The railway station in Old Station Road served refreshments and the landlord of the Engine also held a licence for the Railway Station from 1842 until 1865.

The original Stonebridge Hotel before the extension was added.

David Marks quickly followed by Edward Lowe were the first landlords. The Moore family followed in 1854. Mary Moore is listed in the 1861 census as being a farmer of forty acres as well as the landlord. She was succeeded by Thomas Nathaniel Allen who along with his wife Matilda remained for 41 years.

Several village clubs used to meet at the Engine, including the Oddfellows and the Cricket Club. A plaque on the wall testifies that it was the official quarters of the National Cyclists Union – Birmingham Centre.

The Stonebridge Hotel was originally a small coaching inn on the Birmingham to Coventry Road. The first licensee was Elizabeth Proctor in 1800. She also ran a postal business as well as hiring out horses at 1/3d. per mile. On Elizabeth's death in 1829 as a widow and leaving no will it was left to her son George to take out the letters of administration. The intestate papers were sworn by him on the 4th April of that year stating that the estate was valued at no more than £600 and that he was a victualler by occupation. He had been listed as the licensee since 1826 and he remained at the Hotel for two more years before handing over to the Tabberner family. George then concentrated on his farming interest, he was noted on the voters list of 1833 as farming at Diddington Farm. He died in 1846.

Arriving in 1828 the Tabbener family stayed at the Stonebridge hotel for the next fifty three years. John Tabbener and his wife Elizabeth were in their early twenties when they took over the hotel and they originally came from Balsall Common. They had then moved to Sheldon and had three children when they arrived in Hampton and subsequently had five more.

The Stonebridge Hotel was a popular meeting place for cyclists even before the extension was added. As motoring increased in popularity it also provided a draw for motorists.

North of the Coventry Road and to the west of the Stonebridge Hotel was the Malt Shovel. This was originally just licensed to sell cider and beer. It was first mentioned in a directory of 1860 and was a much smaller establishment than the rather grand Stonebridge Hotel. The exact site of the original Malt Shovel is not known, it was much more humble than the existing Malt Shovel. John Barr, the licensee and his family resided there for some time as a directory of 1860 lists them as occupiers of a beer house. Under the 1830 Beer Act a beer house could only sell cider and beer (as opposed to public houses that could sell wines and spirits as well). A beer house owner only had to apply to the Excise and pay 2 guineas. By

A 1930s photo of the Stonebridge hotel.

1872 when the previous Acts (those for 1834 and 1840 had superceded the above 1830 Act) had been repealed, beer shops came under the jurisdiction of the justices of the peace.

Owned by the Earls of Aylesford, the name Malt Shovel first appeared in the 1872 census. John Barr, like the Gilberts also ran a carpentry business to supplement his income. He was born in Allesley, but his wife Mary was a Hampton girl. They were mine hosts for over 40 years, by which time John was well into his 80s. Their daughter Emma succeeded and carried on trading for a further ten years, her brother Edwin succeeding to the carpentry business.

CHAPTER NINE

Village Sporting Activities

THE EARLY YEARS

The actual year in which sporting activities began in Hampton–in–Arden is difficult to define. On October 16th 1897 the Birmingham News printed a report of a cricket club dinner, attended by fifty gentlemen of the village, held at the Engine Hotel, hosted by Mr Allen, the publican, and chaired by Mr R. J. Bailey, which stated – 'Gentlemen this is the end of our first season, the pitch is not yet in good condition but no doubt will improve with work. Five matches were won, seven drawn and three lost.

Mr Bailey was nominated best batsman and Mr A. King best bowler. The treasurer, Mr J. B. Chandler reported that the expenses for the season was twenty five pounds, leaving a balance of four pounds. All this implies that the Cricket Club began its life in the Spring of 1897. However a copy of a printed programme for an 'Entertainments Evening', in the Girls School, organised by the club shows that the sport was alive and kicking three years earlier in 1894.

Further evidence from a past chairman shows that the club had records of a match played against Solihull as far back as 1870. We can only assume, from these conflicting statements that games of cricket were organised by a group of village residents as early as 1870, but that 'The Hampton-in-Arden Cricket Club' was not formally established until 1897.

An early Cricket Club social occasion.

68

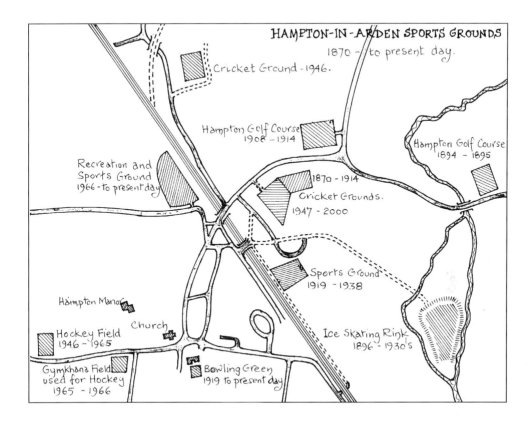

A map showing the area sporting activities in Hampton.

The site of this first cricket club does not appear on any map, but Mr Harvey King, who played cricket for Hampton in the 1920s, placed the ground to the east of Corbett Field, at the back of Old Farm, which is now the end of Lapwing Drive.

Little did they know that this small beginning was to be the foundation of a sporting heritage in the village of Hampton-in-Arden which was to continue, with the exception of two world wars and a world-wide financial crash, until the present day.

On May 13th 1899, a football match was played in Hampton between the Birmingham and Coventry divisions of the Rudge Whitworth Cycle Company. One hundred workers travelled to it, including the Managing Director Mr R.V. Pugh. The match was won by Coventry, five goals to two. The teams then sat down to a *'Capital Meal'* laid on by Mr J. Tall, the publican of the Ring of Bells, followed by a musical evening, which ended at nine o'clock 'in order not to upset the residents of the village'.

A somewhat different atmosphere to the present day!

Although no venue is given, it suggests that the game of football was being played in the village at that time. There was little printed information of this sport until 1902 when it was reported that the Hampton club suffered two defeats, losing to Arden ten goals to nil and to Elmdon three goals to one, and then nothing more until the early 1920s.

Three years later, on May 31st 1902, a meeting was held at the cricket ground where it was decided to form a tennis club. A report in the Birmingham News stated that, - "twenty eight ladies and gentlemen expressed their intention to join". Mrs Newman, Miss Cross, Miss Robertson, Miss Allen (Hon. Sec.) and Messrs H. Burrill, G. Sinclair and F. Wells formed the first committee. Mr Albert Colley offered to purchase nets, posts and other materials and 'A Man', as he was described, was appointed to 'attend' the ground.

On December 8th 1902, a meeting was held at the Engine Hotel to discuss the forming of a Hockey Club.

Some inter-village games had already been played to ensure that sufficient numbers of villagers were interested. Mr R. J. Bailey took the chair. Dr T. H. Brown was proposed as Captain, Mr Bailey as Vice Captain and Mr F. Wells as Hon. Secretary and Treasurer. The first match was to be played in January 1903. Twenty Gentlemen joined.

In the next few years a number of other sporting activities were to be added, but cricket, hockey football and tennis were to become the basic structure of a future amalgamated Sports Club.

THE PRE-FIRST WORLD WAR YEARS, THE CRICKET CLUB

In the first few years, the cricket club went from strength to strength. In 1899, the playing area was doubled in size to over one thousand square yards. In 1900, Hampton played nineteen matches against clubs in the Birmingham area, winning seventeen of them. In 1901 a deputation from the Hampton Junior Cricket Club requested the forming of a second eleven. At the Annual General Meeting, on February 22nd 1902, the President, Mr C. Lea, reported on the club's *"great playing achievements"* in the first five years. It was in this year that the first report of a Ladies cricket team appeared. On August 23rd they scored sixty six runs against the men, who made ninety one. The report did say, however, that "the men bowled and batted left handed".

This annual match between the Ladies and the Gentlemen of the club had now become a regular fixture and in September 1906 it was reported that "the gentlemen played left handed, with broom sticks, and scored 95 runs". Following

A group photograph, possibly taken at one of the Men versus Ladies challenge matches in the early 1900s.

a tea interval, the first nine ladies were bowled out for thirty one runs, but there was a magnificent last wicket stand by Miss Moon, scoring twenty eight, and Miss Palmer, scoring twenty. Miss Palmer was later to be selected to play for Warwickshire Ladies.

A very active social scene existed. Club dinners at the Engine Hotel, smoking concerts and musical evenings, run by Mr Tall of the Ring of Bells, all helped to provide funds. One particular musical evening at the Ring of Bells provided the cricket club with a net profit of twenty six pounds, a large sum of money in 1904.

1906 saw the election of Mr J. Hill as the new President following the death Mr Charles Lea in November of that year. The club provided two silver bowls, in his memory, called the 'Lea Memorial Bowls' to be presented each year to the best batter and best bowler.

At the annual dinner in December 1906, the President reported that "Through the kindness of Lord Aylesford the club has dropped in for a new pitch, and it could not be a better one". The Packington Estate records, most of which were destroyed in a fire in 1980, produces no clear indication of the exact position of this new playing area. This proposed move dragged on for a number of years, the Annual General Meeting in 1907 reported the 'possibility' of moving next season and would incur a cost of one hundred pounds. Concerts, Musical evenings and other social events were held to raise funds.

A team photograph of the Hampton Cricket Club, taken in the early 1920s, together with the Rev. R. C. J. Colthurst and Mr W. A. Frodin, the village schoolmaster.

In 1908 the new ground was reported as, *"being planned and started"*, but it was not until 1910 that the new ground was stated to be *"ready for the 1911 season"*, with one hundred and thirty pounds in hand.

From the end of that season there were no further reports of cricket activities until after the First World War.

THE HOCKEY CLUB

In January 1903 it was reported that there was strong support for the game of hockey, with twenty two 'keen' players. The first match was to be an away match against Bournville. The first Annual General Meeting on September 25th 1903 was presided over by the secretary, Mr Patrick Nathan, Mr Frank Wells, the Captain Mr Jenkins and Vice Captain Dr T. Brown.

By December of this year, due to the increase in membership, a second team had been formed and by the end of 1904 the club had more than doubled its membership. The first team had played 21 matches, won 12, lost 7 and drawn 2. The seconds played 10 matches, won 7, lost 2 and drawn 1.

The introduction of new colours was being discussed at this time. The old colours were not specified, but had been condemned by the members. A decision of blue shorts, purple shirts with white collars and cuffs was made. The President's

Gold Medal for the best player was awarded to Mr Colley, and a Brooch, with the club's initials, was awarded to Miss Allen for her "great interest and activity throughout the season".

The A.G.M. in September 1905 was held at the Engine Hotel, hosted by a new proprietor, John Kibbler, and chaired by Mr Priestley. It was reported that the secretary had been offered a field for a new sports ground "opposite the L.& N.W. Railway goods station on the other side of the railway line". It was never made clear where the

A combined Cricket and Hockey dinner programme signed by members.

first playing area was sited. By the end of September the new ground had been drained, and new goal posts erected at a cost of twenty pounds. By 1906, Hampton was being reported as one of the leading Midland Hockey Clubs. G. Mobberley (goalkeeper) and H. Tickler were both individually named and received high praise for their game, both being selected as reserves for the County in November of that year.

By 1907, the Hampton ground was used as a venue for County matches and between 1907 and 1913, three Warwickshire hockey matches were played on this pitch, which was described as "one of the finest in the county". In 1910, the Hampton ground was further honoured by being selected for a match between the Midland Counties and the West, which ended in a two-all draw.

On November 11th 1908 Warwickshire beat Leicestershire by eighteen goals to one at Hampton. G. Mobberley of Hampton played in goal. On November 2nd 1911, Warwickshire played Northamptonshire winning by ten goals to nil. H. W. Tickler of Hampton played in this match and was also reported as playing in goal in all County matches throughout the 1912-1913 seasons.

On November 20th 1913, Hampton hosted a match between Warwickshire and Northamptonshire, which the home county won by ten goals to one. A resident of Hampton, Mr. H. M. Kesterton, played for Hampton at this time, was a full time player for Warwickshire and the Midlands and was later selected to play for England. He lived at 5 The Grove, Hampton-in-Arden, later owned by Mr Norman Fowles, the President of the Hockey Club from 1959 to 1968.

COUNTY FIXTURES

25.11.1896
Warwickshire (5) v Worcestershire (2)
(First ever County match played in the Midlands)

3.12.1906
Warwickshire (7) v Leicestershire (1)
G. T. Moberley (Hampton)

29.11.1907
Warwickshire (5) v Northamptonshire (4)
G. T. Moberley (Hampton)

11.11.1908
Warwickshire (18) v Leicestershire (1)
G.T. Moberley (Hampton)   PLAYED AT HAMPTON-IN-ARDEN

9.1.1910
Midland Counties (2) v The West (2)
                         PLAYED AT HAMPTON-IN-ARDEN

2.11.1911
Warwickshire (10) v Northamptonshire (0)
H.W. Tickler (Hampton)   PLAYED AT HAMPTON-IN-ARDEN

1912-1913 Season
Warwickshire (8)   v   Northamptonshire (0)
Warwickshire (7)   v   Derbyshire (1)
Warwickshire (10) v   Shropshire (0)
Warwickshire (3)   v   Staffordshire (2)
Warwickshire (4)   v   Surrey (1)
H. W. Tickler played Goalkeeper in all these matches

20.11.1913
Warwickshire (10) v Northamptonshire (1)
H. M. Kesterton (Hampton)   PLAYED AT HAMPTON-IN-ARDEN

Left - Hampton Hockey team in 1922, taken in front of the converted railway coach. N. Colthurst, the son of the vicar, is standing on the right. Right - A list of Warwickshires County Hockey fixtures showing a number played on the Hampton ground.

TENNIS CLUB

Following the first report of the formation of the Tennis Club in 1902, no further information appears until 1906, when it was reported that a Tennis Club dance had been held, on February 3rd at the Assembly Room of the Ring of Bells Inn. Presumably, in the early years, this was a village club, used by the residents, for social family tennis with no formal matches or outside activities. On April 7th 1906 a Tennis Club Annual General Meeting was held at the Engine Hotel. Miss Allen was the Chairman, Mr B. Tickler the secretary and a committee formed by Mr Cross, Miss Palmer, Mr F. Wells, Mr H. S. Henderson and Mr B. Nathan. The balance of funds was £10 13s 10d. A tournament was to be arranged, on the American system.

The Annual General Meeting on April 6th 1907, was held at the home of Mr A. J. Priestley. The tournament results were reported, Miss Cecily Peploe won the President's Prize and Mr R. T. Scott the Club Prize. The balance of funds now was £17 4s 10d. Two courts were said to be in good working order and two special matches were being arranged. The club was obviously broadening its horizons.

In 1908, the club dance was held at the Stonebridge Hotel and at the Annual General Meeting in this year Mr Priestley, the new President, reported that a third court had been added. Like both the cricket and hockey clubs the tennis club was

Hampton Tennis Club, taken in 1908 in the front of the clubhouse, converted from a railway Pullman Coach.

discussing a move to another site. The cost of eighty pounds to re-lay new courts was considered to be too costly and the decision was deferred.

On January 16th 1909 a 'Tennis Club Ball' was held at 'Ye Olde Hotel' at Stonebridge. It was called the 'Calico Dress Ball'. The ladies were all dressed in white and red calico, and the gentlemen in white duck suits.

A photograph, taken in the summer season shows a group of Edwardian clad tennis players sitting outside the clubhouse. This was a converted Pullman railway carriage, donated or bought from the London & North Western Railway, with a veranda and canopy extension along the front. This carriage was set on fire by German incendiaries in the 1940 blitz and was later used as a hay store by the local farmer into the 1950s.

The last report, published prior to the First World War was a tennis match result between Hampton and Blyth (Coleshill), in June 1910, which Hampton won.

THE HAMPTON-IN-ARDEN ATHLETIC AND SOCIAL CLUB

Two reports from early Cricket Club dinners, show the first thoughts being given to the amalgamation of the individual clubs. On December 13th 1902, Dr T. H. Brown stated that – *'the cricket club now embraced hockey, tennis, football and bowls'*, and on March 28th 1903 a sub-committee was established to consider the formation of a joint sports club with a new Gymnasium and Club Room.

Hampton football team, winners of the Mitchells and Butler Shield, taken outside the front of the Fentham Club in 1948. The President, Colonel Humphries, is seated in the centre.

There were no more reports from this sub-committee with thoughts of integration until 1919. In the years following the end of the First World War, and the slow return to normality, the individual sporting activities were finally amalgamated into The Hampton-in-Arden Athletic and Sports Club. This was an event which was to be repeated, in a similar way, fifty three years later.

Some new activities were being added at this time. The game of bowls commenced at the Fentham Club on August 30th 1919 with a match against Selly Park, which Hampton won by 45 points. The bowling green at the rear of the Fentham Club was well used between the two world wars, and particularly by the British Legion members after the second World War. It is still active today. Small Bore Rifle shooting was held in a 'Village Hut' and a Swimming Club was formed.

Regular reports now began to appear in the Birmingham News of sports activities. On June 12th 1920 the cricket section played its first match against Southalls Cricket Club and won by 72 runs. In July Mr Cleverley and Miss Frodin organised an American Tournament for the tennis section. In this year we also see the beginning of a Ladies Hockey Section. On September 18th a group of Hampton ladies formed a ladies section under the chairmanship of Miss Ethel

King, who later became the village postmistress, captain Miss L. Frodin and vice captain Miss H. Wooley. The first match was an inter-club mixed match to be played on October 2nd.

On April 30th 1921, an A.G.M. of the Athletic & Social Club was held at the Ring of Bells, the landlord at that time was Mr W. H. Jones. The President, Mr J. Rollason, reported that the funds were not good, the pavilion was in poor shape and the repairs and decorations had caused a drain on the club's finances. A request was to be made to the Fentham Trust for financial help.

The chairmen of the sports sections, Mr H. King (Men's Hockey), Miss Frodin (Ladies Hockey), Mr W. W. Relph (Football), Mr Cleverley (Tennis), Mr H. Jones (Cricket), Mr S. Maylett (Swimming), and Mr R. C. Colley (Social) gave progress reports but no details were published. Inclusive subscriptions were raised to thirty shillings.

The swimming section was still active, Mr J. Dutton becoming the new chairman in May 1921, and in the same month a report from the tennis section A.G.M. stated that there were now four courts in operation and that boundary nets had been obtained and wire fencing erected to keep out the sheep. The hockey section played a mixed inter club match on Boxing morning, December 26th 1922 in fancy dress. Mr Shipton, landlord of the Engine Hotel, was the referee in a clown costume and Mr Harvey Burrill dressed as a sheik. This boxing morning fancy dress match was re-commenced in the mid-nineteen fifties, played against the cricket club, and continued for some years.

On May 5th 1923, at the Sports Club A.G.M., Mr H. Baker, chairman of the hockey section reported great successes and that they had not been beaten at home since the 1920 season, but although reports from the individual sports sections continued to attract great popularity and enthusiasm, there were signs of increasing financial problems. Subscriptions were down, leaving a bank balance of only eleven pounds. A loss was made on the last two club dances, a clear indication that people were looking a little more carefully into their personal finances. The country was heading towards the beginning of worldwide financial problems and the final crisis of a financial crash was yet to come.

On April 28th 1924, an extraordinary general meeting was called, with one motion on the agenda being, 'That the Hampton-in-Arden Athletic and Social Club shall be disbanded' Mr W. Frodin, Major Phillips and Mr Wayne headed a special sub committee to formally wind up the Sports Club and it was agreed that the individual clubs should be reformed and decide their own future. At this time football, swimming and ladies hockey ceased to exist. Some cricket and hockey match results are noted up to 1929, but they are few.

The Tennis Club did not appear to hold match fixtures and inter club events were obviously not considered worthy of mention. Comments from the older villagers who remember the years prior to the last war show that there were still some football matches being played, and the Tennis club was very active up to 1938.

If we turn back in time a little we find that there were other sporting activities in the village, that were not part of this amalgamated sports club.

On March 28th 1898 the Hampton branch of the Forest of Arden Lodge of Oddfellows held their first Athletic Sports Day in the village. At 10.45am, they processed from The Engine Hotel to the Church, led by the Solihull Brass Band, where the Reverend Morris held a service. They then returned to The Engine, where sixty sat to dinner, the Rev. Morris taking the chair. The company then adjourned to the Hampton cricket ground, at 2.45pm when the sports events commenced. During the event, reported in typical journalese of the day, The Walbrook Glee Singers, made up of Messrs Sparks, King, Seymour and Sapset, rendered various 'glees' in a very high class manner.

Sideshows and teas were available to the 350 spectators attending on that rather rainy afternoon who watched the prizes being distributed by Mrs Morris, the wife of the Vicar. This very popular event was reported regularly, and in great detail, in the Birmingham News between 1900 and 1914, listing all events and the winners.

Oddfellows Athletic Sports Day - March 28th 1898.	
150 yards handicap (Girls)	Elsie King(1) Rose Mills(2) M Whitehead (3)
120 yards handicap	F.Neale (1) J.Kimberley (2) T Llewellyn (3)
200 yards (Lodge members over 35)	W King (1) G Varnun (2) T Whitehead (3)
150 yards handicap (Boys)	H Wheeler (1) S Homer (2) A Moreton (3)
¼ mile flat handicap	W Galloway (1) J Kimberely (2) B Hubbard (3)
100 yards handicap (Girls)	Gertie Varnun(1) Jessie Clark(2) Edith Morgan (3)
75 yards Sack Race	G Nield (1) N Nield(2) C Harris (3)
75 yards handicap (Boys under 7)	C Wilkes (1) A Wilkes (2) A Bailey (3)
¼ mile handicap	W Felton (1) G E Varnun (2) A E Galloway (3)
100 yards handicap (Boys)	G Lee (1) W Hill (2) F Whitehead (3)
100 yards Slow bicycle race	A Lloyd (1) A E Galloway (2) S R Peploe (3)
150 yards handicap (Hurdle)	W Peach (1) F Cook (2) H Nield (3)
Bun & Jockey Race (Open)	C & T Nield (1) F Field & A Coton (2)
½ mile obstacle race (Lodge members under 35)	A E Galloway (1) D Galloway (2) C Harris (3)
220 yards handicap (Lodge members under 35)	W Stilgoe (1) B Hubbard (2) J Poole (3)
1 mile steeplechase (Radius)	G E Varnun (1) B Hubbard (2) W Felton (3)

Results of the Oddfellows Sports event in 1898.

THE GOLF CLUB

Over the years there were two golf course sites, in or near the village, both named Hampton Golf Club. The following information has been taken from 'Celebrating a Centenary, North Warwicks Golf Club 1894–1994', written by Mrs Shirley Whitney.

On June 1st 1894, twenty ladies and gentlemen gathered in the boys schoolroom in Hampton-in-Arden to form a new golf club. Mr Edward Peynton was elected as the President, together with a Secretary and a Treasurer who were not named. A committee was formed and a 'Small Rule Book' was produced. One remaining copy of this is said to be in the possession of the North Warwicks club. A local farmer, Mr J. M. Cattell of Patrick Farm, rented an area of his ground for this first golf course. Farmers were going through difficult times and were always looking for other sources of income from their land. No record of payment is known, but at about this time Olton Golf Club was paying five pounds a year to Langley Hall Farm for a field

The exact position of the Patrick Farm field, where the first club was built, is not reported, but local knowledge places it on the Meriden side of the River Blythe, just outside the Parish boundary, opposite the farm. There was little delay to the proceedings and play must have started immediately. It is reported that Mr A. Edmunds won the 'Silver Cup' in a club competition in July 1894. The club stayed at this location for only one year, as in 1895 they were offered a piece of land by Lord Aylesford which was originally used as his private race course, known then as 'Meriden Common'. It was later renamed as 'Meriden Links'.

Dates and names inscribed on the silver cup and those in the original rule book of the Hampton Golf Club, are identical, thus proving that that the Hampton club was the forerunner of what was later to become 'North Warwickshire Golf Club'.

There was, however, another Hampton Golf Club which started out as a, five hole course, built on a field belonging to Mr Corbett, a Birmingham industrialist, in the corner of Diddington Lane and Meriden Road. A house called Fairway, on Diddington Lane is thought to be sited across the original entrance of this club. The course was designed and laid out by Mr Hunt in 1908-9 and the club remained active, and well attended, for the next few years.

In July 1911 the original five hole course was extended to a form new nine hole course and in August 1912, Mr G. Senior won the monthly medal, with a net score of 65. The Annual General Meeting held in March 1913, at the Engine Hotel, was attended by 108 members. Mr R. J. Bailey was the president and the committee formed by Mr C. Still, Mr Frodin, Mr F. Cross, Mr H. Burrill, Mr S. E. Cox, S. Ayres and W. Jones. The September monthly medal in this year was won by Mr A. Burton with a net score of 70. This Hampton Golf Club was finally disbanded in 1914.

THE HAMPTON-IN-ARDEN OUTDOOR ICE SKATING RINK

This was the regular winter sporting event that brought great distinction, and attracted large numbers of skaters, and spectators to the village of Hampton. The first indication of this activity was sometime in 1896, but the first positive report appeared in the Birmingham News on December 11th 1897, which stated that, *"The Hampton skating rink has now been constructed, in a field, about ten minutes walk from the Railway Station. The field is twenty acres in extent and seventeen acres of this are flooded to a maximum depth of two feet five inches. The flooded area has a good promenade surrounding it and is floodlit with oil lamps for skating at night".* It is not clear whether the project was officially organised by the local council or run privately by a group of residents. We do know that Mr Cattell, of Patrick Farm, provided or leased, the area of land and that the surrounding board walk was constructed by the local timber firm, Wyckham Blackwell. In the following years, a succession of reports in the newspaper regularly advertised this event. It appears that the winters at this time were always cold enough to provide sufficient frost for skating. On January 28th 1898, it merely stated that the rink was flooded and lit for use, but on December 23rd 1899, a more detailed report appeared.

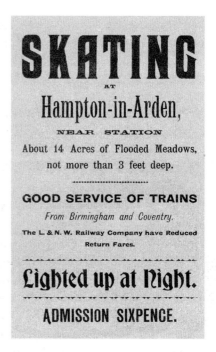

A handbill advertising the Hampton Ice Rink.

"Hampton skating rink is now flooded over an area of fourteen acres. Admission 6p per session, (Season ticket 5s). Half the funds will be given to the Daily Mail Reservists Fund". This was a Boer War veterans' fund set up by the Birmingham Daily newspaper. Arrangements have been made with the London, North Western Railway to provide cheap fares from Birmingham and Coventry (1s return). Reports appeared most winters in the following years, the last one in February 1919, stating that *"Skating is now in operation on Parkers Pool and Mercote Mill Pool".* A number of villagers who lived in Hampton before the last war can remember walking down the footpath on the east side of the railway line and across the fields to skate on this flooded area in the late nineteen thirties. Ordnance survey maps of this area still show the raised promenade of this rink in the marsh between the River Blythe and a narrow brook called The Drain.

POST SECOND WORLD WAR PERIOD

In the years following the Second World War, the level of sport that existed in the early 1900s was to be repeated, with the introduction of a number of other sporting activities, and eventually forming another amalgamated sports club, with just one difference. On this occasion the Cricket Club, which had previously been the foundation of the early sports club in 1919, was to remain independent. The first record that we have of sport being played, after the war, is a brief set of minutes, handwritten on a page torn from an exercise book, dated February 6th 1946. Norman Pegg made the proposal that a Hockey Club be formed, stating that twenty two members of the village were interested. A meeting was held with Owen T. George, Headmaster of Fentham School as chairman and Muriel Pegg as secretary. Those present agreed to meet the next day, on the field, for a first trial game.

Quoting from a letter written by Muriel Pegg – *"My brother Norman and I approached Ted Jones of Home Farm in Bickenhill Lane, and leased a field adjacent to the Solihull Road for one pound a season. We cleared the ground of cow manure, borrowed a tennis marking machine for the lines, made flags and corner posts, begged old curtain rails from Fentham hall to make goal posts, all just in time for the first match"*. If anyone can claim to be the true founders of post war hockey, it has to be the 'Family Pegg'.

It was in the 1947/48 seasons, when a group of young men, recently de-mobbed from the forces, returned to the village, and building on this early foundation, re-established sport in Hampton as we know it today. Dennis Butler, whose father was a partner in the Wyckham Blackwell Timber Company, together with John Lovegrove, advertised around the village for interest in forming a cricket club. Stan Butler, brother of Dennis, and Norman Pegg pursued local interest in Hockey.

By this time a football club had been formed, based in the Fentham Club. A photograph of the team exists, taken outside the entrance of the club, after winning the Mitchells and Butler Shield in 1948-49. Shown with them is the President, Colonel Humphries, who lived at Church House Farm, Tom Oakley, the club captain and Mr Margettes, the Fentham Club steward.

Although very few records of this club can be found, the game remained popular in the village and is still very active today, notable wins are the Carnation Premier League, the Midlands Sunday Invitation Cup and the Keeley Cup. Information taken from the village Millennium Book records the addition of two junior teams, under 7s and 14s and over 80 junior members being coached.

THE BOWLING CLUB

The game of crown green bowls was still active on the bowling green, in the grounds at the rear of the Fentham Club. Records from the minutes show that the game remained active throughout the war, and continued for a number of

The bowlers of the Fentham Institute taken in the late 1920s.

years. In the late 1990s, mainly caused by a reduced membership of the club, the use of the bowling green declined. In the year 2000, a Probus Bowls Tournament was organised which then became an annual event. Every August, the Bowls Challenge is played between the Probus Club and the Women's Institute, for the coveted 'Rolling Pin'.

From this event a small group of Probus and W.I. members, headed by Frank Earnshaw, advertised a village meeting to promote interest in the re-forming of a Bowls Club. A constitution was established in October 2002 and the first general meeting of members in march 2003. By the end of its first full season, the newly formed Hampton Bowls Club had increased its membership and the green is once again well used.

THE BADMINTON CLUB

In 1949, Paul Randall and Mrs Barnsley founded a Badminton Club. It was played in the Fentham Hall on three afternoons and two evenings each week. At its peak, membership reached forty. It was affiliated to the All England Badminton Club and in 1983 the Ladies team came top of division one of the Solihull league. In 1987, a junior section was formed, but unfortunately in 1990, through lack of support, the club was dissolved.

THE HAMPTON-IN-ARDEN HORSE SHOW & GYMKHANA

There is a nice little story of an English pilot, and former prisoner of war, who told Mrs Barnsley about the poor distribution of Red Cross parcels in prisoner-of-war camps and could something be done to help raise funds? So, in 1944, the seed was set for the beginning of the Hampton-in-Arden Horse Show & Gymkhana, started for this one purpose of aiding the International Red Cross. It started on the same field that eventually became the first hockey ground in 1946, on the right hand side of the Solihull Road. It was moved, sometime in the mid-1950s, to the field at the corner of Solihull Road and Eastcote Lane. The Olympic Silver Medallist, Ann Moore, competed in her first open event on this ground. In 1969, the year of the Silver Jubilee celebrations, three hundred horses and their riders took part in a two-day event. There were a hundred and forty entries in the Dog Show and over 1,700 spectators attended over the weekend.

The gymkhana nearly folded in 1973, but John Chapman, took over as Chairman, together with a new committee, and the show continued under the new name of 'The Hampton-in-Arden District Horse Show & Country Fair'. The 46th show in September 1989 made a loss of £200, and as it was costing £4,000 to stage, it was decided that the show could not continue.

THE CRICKET CLUB

The Cricket Club was re-started in the summer of 1947 in a field almost opposite The Grove off Old Station Road, which was thought to be used, during the war as an 'Ack-Ack' site. Recollections of John Lovegrove, a founder member, said that after spending some time preparing the pitch on this ground, and before any games were actually played there, a more suitable piece of land had been offered by Mr Corbett, Bunty Taylor's father, at the back of Old Farm. This was to be known throughout the life of the club as 'Corbetts Field'.

No finances were available to pay for professional preparation of the ground, so those early members rolled up their sleeves and filled in ditches, removed trees and extended boundaries to provide a suitable playing area. Pigsties were turned into toilets. With the provision of donations from village residents and the help of Wyckham Blackwell, the old barn was stripped out and turned into a pavilion. For years this pavilion was also used as a headquarters and sorting office for the village Christmas Post. It was like Fort Knox, closely guarded by 'Peter the Post'.

This building received some level of fame, when it was proudly listed alongside the Worcestershire and Warwickshire county pavilions, in a book written by the brother of songwriter Tim Rice. His comment was "Hampton-in-Arden's atmospheric, ivy covered, red brick pavilion is probably the oldest building I have discovered being used for cricketing purposes".

In the period of the 1950s and 1960s, Hampton was never in the first league of cricket and was usually matched against the second XI of major clubs. At one time there was some thoughts of forming a third team, but its ground was not large enough. This brought about thoughts of moving to a larger site and in the 1970s they looked at a field in Diddington Lane and another at the rear of the Malt Shovel in Barston. There was some discussion at this time of forming a sports complex, and the Hockey Club was invited to join them at the ground in Barston. In the 1980s, there was even some consideration being given to a move to the village recreation ground.

The club's fixtures were mainly Midlands friendly games and Sunday Six-a-Side games played between other village organisations, but in the early 1970s the club took a stride forward and joined the Warwickshire & Staffordshire League. The ground was used, on occasions, by teams formed from the Birmingham Clergy and Doctors. A match was once played against the cast of My Fair Lady when the production was on tour at a Birmingham theatre.

The club was probably best known for its open village festivities. In the summer they held a number of village barbecues and an annual 'Donkey Derby' with racing for adults and children. This was eventually replaced by a go-kart racing event, together with sulky and chariot races fought out by various village teams. The most notable cricket club event of the year was Bonfire Night. An enormous fire topped with a life-size Guy, together with food, drink and a firework display. This was one of the highlights in the village calendar.

The cricket club remained on Corbett Field until its recent collapse because of a lack of players in Hampton. The few remaining members took the club and amalgamated with Solihull Cricket Club at their Marsh Lane ground in Solihull.

THE HOCKEY CLUB

The Hockey Club, which was to become the largest of the new sports activities and the eventual founder of the new sports complex, remained on the Solihull Road ground until 1965. The original subscription cost 6d per game, later becoming an annual fee of 10 shillings, non-earners 5 shillings and members of H. M. Forces 1 shilling per game. These were the days of post war austerity, clothing coupons had to be found to purchase club kit. Jerseys were priced at £10 3s 9d per dozen and socks at 4s 8d a pair.

Visiting teams arrived by train or car, if they could obtain petrol, and they changed at the Church Hall, which was then at the rear of the vicarage near Fentham Road, and walked to the ground. Dances and whist drives were organised to help boost funds. At one social event in 1949, a net profit of £30 10s was made, a large boost to the club funds at that time. This year also saw the beginning of an association with the Hampton Gymkhana. Members of the hockey club volunteered to work in the Ring and the car park, and continued to do so until the demise of the Gymkhana in 1989.

By the 1950 season there were three teams, a ladies, a men's and a mixed team with a total playing strength of forty four – twenty three ladies and twenty one men. The colour of the kit was changed from blue and white to the present quartered green and black.

The whist drives were eventually replaced by two annual club events, the dinner dance, always fully attended, held first at the 'Good Companions' in Yardley, later moving to Forest Hotel in Dorridge, then to the Greswolde in Knowle and finally for a number of years at The Manor at Meriden. The most popular event of the year, and another highlight in the village calendar was the Boxing Night Dance, held at the Fentham Hall.

By the early 1960s negotiations were under way with the Parish Council for the provision of hockey and football pitches, and a pavilion, to be sited on the village recreation ground in Shadowbrook Lane. This was the beginning of great changes in village sport. On February 1st 1965 the Parish Council gave

Moorcroft & Sons permission to start the building of the clubhouse at a cost of £4,500. Under the chairmanship of Robin Watkin, a House Committee was formed to organise the opening event and on September 11th 1965, the Hockey Club Pavilion and ground, was officially opened by Martin Kesterton, now in his eighties, who had played for Hampton, Warwickshire and England in the 1920s. The club increased in playing strength, fielding up to five men's, three ladies, a mixed and Sunday teams. Both the men and the ladies achieved great success in the Midlands Hockey League. Over the hundred years between 1902 and 2002, 34 ladies and 21 men of the Hampton Club have been selected to play for Warwickshire, and from that total 24 for Midlands Counties and nine for England.

The early 1960s saw the beginning of great change, and the increase in sporting activities in the village. George Fish, Chairman of the Parish Council at that time, approached Robin Watkin with the comment *"I think we should start a tennis club in the village"*. Robin later commented, *"I didn't realise until much later that this was the 'Royal We'"*. With an enormous amount of help from Peter and Pat Adams, over the next year local clubs in the midland area were visited for information and details of courts, surface types, suitable construction companies and costs were put together.

In May 1966, an open village meeting was held in the upstairs room of the Congregational Church. Eighty people attended that meeting and an organising committee was formed, with Robin Watkin as Chairman, Doreen Abbot, (now Trumper), as Secretary and Peter Adams as Treasurer. Donations collected at the end of that meeting raised £1,350 and the new committee had full approval to begin planning a new tennis club.

After lengthy negotiations with the Parish Council, the club was finally opened, two years later, on April 6th 1968 by the President of the Warwickshire Lawn Tennis Association with a demonstration match played by, Jaraslav Drobny and Bobby Howe. A total of two hundred and twenty members joined in that first year and the club has remained very active, with considerable coaching of junior players. From 1972 onwards there were other changes being made. Discussions were under way for a complete renovation of the original clubhouse. Two squash courts were planned as an extension to the rear and a tennis club lounge, at the side, overlooking the courts.

In 1973, the Hockey Club sent out invitations to the Football, Tennis and Squash clubs to form an amalgamated Sports Club, and a new constitution would be written. By 1974 the Sports Club building was completed, on September 13th the new Squash Club was officially opened, and so a Sports Club was formed, in the village, for the second time in its sporting history, with just one difference. On this occasion, the Cricket Club continued to bat alone.

In more recent years the game of Racquet Ball has been added as an alternative to Squash. A Boules Piste was laid down outside the front of the clubhouse. Sixteen teams, in two divisions, formed from other village organisations and private groups play in a summer league with a grand final in September. Probably the last sporting activity to arrive in the village was Netball. The Hampton Harriers Netball Club founded by three young ladies in 1998. According to the Hampton Millennium Book, they first trained at the George Fentham School and by the year 2000, membership was on the increase and match results were encouraging.

One fact does become apparent when we look at the records of the sporting clubs. Over the considerable number of years of playing activity on the field there has always been a strong link with a social scene, either for club funding or just for continued enjoyment.

Probably the greatest change in the sporting activity is the age range of the players. In the early 1900s sport was mainly an adult activity, but today ideas and attitudes have changed. Children from early school age are being coached and encouraged to play sport, and members of sports clubs, like Hampton, are to be applauded for their hard work and involvement, with the coaching sessions of children from across the Parish.

The Hampton Sports complex has now been re-designed and a new Recreation Trust has been formed. With the aid of public grants, charity and private donations a large sum of money has been provided to fund the re-building of the sports activities. In May 2004 the entire layout of the Recreation Field, Sports ground was re-designed to include a new All Weather Hockey Pitch, the re-siting of football pitches and tennis courts, and extensions to the clubhouse changing rooms. Once again in its one hundred and thirty year history there is a new beginning for sporting activities in Hampton.

CHAPTER TEN

Village Businesses

The first reference to a shop in the village appears in the tithe apportionment of 1841. The Tithe Map shows all the land within the parish and the accompanying apportionment lists the amount of tithes due. This shows that West End cottage was owned by Thomas Buggins, who lived in it and ran a butcher's shop there. The only other shop mentioned is a "smith's shop", believed to be a wheelwright's shop, a short distance away. However by the 1850s the village contains two carriers, two blacksmiths (one a woman, Mrs Sarah Jones of Stonebridge), two saddlers, two boot and shoemakers, a brickmaker and a wheelwright as well as 12 farmers. Two of the farmers have secondary occupations, one is a farmer and carrier and the other a farmer and coal merchant. John Gilbert, landlord of the Ring of Bells public house is also a carpenter and George Jennings of the White Lion is also a butcher. The three carriers all state that they go to Birmingham every Thursday. There is a second butcher, William Orton and two shopkeepers. One, Benjamin Butler, has the corner shop which at this time incorporates the Post Office, and George Chandler but we do not know where his shop was.

By the 1860s the village also boasts a tailor, William Brown and there are 3 shoemakers in the village although the term cordwainer is more commonly used. The population is given as 590 but this almost certainly includes two remote parts of the parish, Kinwalsey and Nuthurst as well as Catherine de Barnes.

GROCERS AND GREENGROCERS

The Burrill family ran a grocery business in Hampton for over a hundred years. This business was started by Frederick Burrill who was born in Boston, Lincolnshire, married a Birmingham girl and opened a shop in 1863 when he was 24. The Burrills appear in the 1871 census as Frederick, aged 32, his wife Selina, 31, and their three children: twins, Thomas and George, 7, and John, 5. The two older boys were born in Birmingham but John was born in Hampton. Their shop was at the end of a row of cottages known as Shepherds Row in what was

John Burrill's shop in the row of cottages just before the bend in the present Shadow Brook Lane.

Bickenhill Lane. This is now Shadow Brook Lane and the cottages, demolished in the 1960s, were on the roadside where the Fentham Green bungalows are now. On the 1881 census the Burrills had an additional son, Harry who was 6 years old. George appears to have left home, he would have been 17 by then, but Thomas was still there and was described as a confectioner's shopman. John, 15, was listed as an office boy. At the time of the 1891 census the business was being run by Frederick's widow and she had two sons at home: John, now a commercial traveller and Harry, a clerk.

During this period there was also a grocer's shop at the top of the village, now known as the Corner Shop at the junction of the High Street and Marsh Lane. The first known shopkeeper was a Benjamin Butler who between 1854 and 1864 was a grocer and provision merchant. The 1871 census shows this to be a grocer's shop run by Samuel Wood. He was there until 1874. On the 1881 census the shop was run by William Ratherham, described as a chemist and druggist. From 1888 to 1900 the shop was run by Thomas Garlick who called himself a grocer and draper. The Garlick family later emigrated to America.

Memories of Hampton describe the shop at the turn of the 19th century as a chemist's shop as well as a grocer's shop but from the advertisements placed in the Chronicle it was not a chemist as we know it today as it appeared to have sold patent medicines. It was also the Post Office which in those days included the telegraph office. Because Sir Frederick Peel did not approve of a Post Office being located there the postmaster, Robert Thompson, opened a new Post Office across the road in about 1894. This building is now known as the Old Post Office.

The present corner shop taken at the end of the 19th Century with its entrance in Marsh Lane. On the right is Canterbury House.

At that time the entrance to the Corner Shop was in Marsh Lane. Around the time of the First World War the Burrill family took over the shop, which from then until well after the Second World War was known as Burrill's Top Shop. This distinguished it from the shop in Shepherds Row which was referred to as the Bottom Shop. Between 1914 and 1921 the two shops were run by Frederick's Burrill's son John and after his death, from about 1924 to 1940, they were managed by John's widow, Edith, who had been his second wife. By 1941 the business was being run by E. Burrill & H. Burrill. The H. is for Harry, John's brother. After the war the business was run by Harvey

Now a private house at 106 High Street, this photograph, taken just before the First World War, shows the grocery shop run by C. Reeves, later on called The Village Stores.

Burrill, John's son by his first wife. After Harvey Burrill's death the shop was initially run under the name of "Burrill's Stores" but the name was dropped and the shop has since been operated by a number of different people.

Another grocery shop in the Hampton was the Village Stores. Located at 106 High Street it was adapted from a cottage. The shop existed from before the First World War when it was run by a C. Reeves, described as a Grocer, Provision Merchant and General Dealer.

West End Cottage when it was occupied by Frank Ashbourn.

In 1917 the Village Stores was acquired by a Mrs Martin whose husband ran a painting and decorating business whilst she ran the shop. According to the Women's Institute scrapbook, produced in 1956, this shop was started in 1881 by a widow who lived on a pension of 7s 6d per week paid to her by the George Fentham Charity.

"*She decided to eke out her allowance by making toffee to sell to the children on their way to the Girls' School almost opposite, and in the tiny cottage room, bare except for one three legged table, for the widow was very poor, began the first shop on that site. After the lady died the shop was taken over by a family with ideas for a little more enterprise. They started growing flowers which they took to Birmingham and sold probably in the street market. What a lovely thought - spring flowers from Hampton, marketed to bring a breath of the countryside to industrial Birmingham. But their enterprise did not end there. With the money saved from the flower trade they bought jars of sweets to sell in the village shop which became a valuable asset as time went on. The business changed hands several times until, in the early part of this century it was taken over by a chemist. He only survived three years. This kind of business was very bad. However the old widow's shop eventually passed into the hands of the Martins*".

This comment was updated in 1981 to read as follows,

"The small shop in the High Street just above the Engine generally known as "Martins" still sells groceries, cigarettes and sweets, but what was once its cottage garden has been concreted over and is now filled with benches of fruit and vegetables, plants and cut flowers under a stripped awning. Thus the little shop that once used to sell garden flowers to Birmingham now imports flowers from Birmingham market to sell to those living in the village".

Since 1981 the shop has moved further up the High Street and is now next to the Wine Shop which was for many years the local butchers.

BUTCHERS

As mentioned above, the first butcher's shop was in West End Cottage on the corner of Solihull Road and the road to Knowle. It is not known when this ceased to be a butcher's but it later became the home and base of operations for a florist called Frank Ashbourn and then a private house.

Later on the end house in the pargeted cottages became a butcher's shop (hence the name Butcher's Road). The cottages were built in 1868 and in the 1871 census the end cottage was occupied by Enoch Homer, an agricultural labourer. In the 1881 census the occupant is Frank Harper, a 39 year old butcher who was still there in 1891. In that census one of his sons, also called Frank, is

The Butcher's Shop on the corner of Butchers Road. Photograph taken in 1925.

listed as a butcher's assistant. An advertisement in 1941 for H. L. Large, butcher, gives his address as 12 High Street but the shop almost certainly was on the corner of Butchers Road. The numbering of the High Street seems to have varied from time to time. Early records indicate that coming down the hill from the corner shop the numbering did not start until after the White Lion.

Memories of the village for the period 1914 to 1921 say that A. H. Eborall was the village butcher. The Parish Magazine, between 1921 to 1932 contains an advert saying he was a family butcher who had fresh supplies of English meat daily. A. H. was not the first Eborall to be a butcher in Hampton as a Cornelius Eborall ran a shop next to the Ring of Bells and a photograph shows him standing outside his shop with the meat hanging outside. This was during the early 1900s.

In 1933 there is H. F. King in the shop on the corner of Butchers Road advertising as a family butcher with a "Coldair" electric refrigerator and offering home-killed meat. He was there until 1935 and was followed by L. J. Large who advertised as a high class family butcher, waiting on families daily. He was followed by a Mr Tuckey, another Mr Eborall and then, the final butcher to occupy the site, Mr Dennis McGauley who ceased trading in 1986.

For many years the Butcher's Road shop had a slaughter house at the rear and a field where the animals were kept prior to slaughter.

THE HIGH STREET

Down the High Street from the Corner Shop is the present hairdressers (which retains the name Number One from when it operated out of the rear of number one Station Road). The earliest known use of this shop is as a draper's run by Miss Dorothy Burrill. She was followed by a Miss Frampton and then, in 1937, it was taken by a Mrs Ida Mills who ran it until 1964 when her niece Mrs Margaret Sargent took it over. Since then the shop has had a number of occupants including an antiques dealer and an optician.

It is not known when the present sandwich shop in the High Street started operating as a bakery. There was a baker running a business there in 1881. The building (which now houses bedrooms for the White Lion) was divided into four parts. First, as it is approached from the rear of the present Post Office, was the working part of the bakery. It was a two-storey building, the upper part being a flour store and below was where the dough was mixed. At the back was the oven which extended to the stable for the horse used to pull the delivery vehicle. This vehicle was kept in the final part of the building. Bread was delivered within the village and to surrounding villages. It was not until after the Second World War that a motorised vehicle was used.

In 1891 the baker was a Joseph Elson who was followed by a Harold Poole. Arthur Rouse arrived in 1929, having previously been a baker in Stratford. He brought with him Len Timms to work in the bakery and who later married a Hampton girl and settled in the village. Mr Rouse advertised his business as "baker, confectioner and corn merchant". He made wedding, birthday and christening cakes to order and all kinds fancy cakes were produced daily.

The present Post Office is first recorded as being a shop in 1932 when William Henry Jones is a purveyor of cooked meats. In 1939 Mrs Emily May Morris, who lived in Shepherds Row and operated as a newsagent from a little shanty, moved in to what is now the Post Office. She advertised as "newsagent, stationer, tobacconist and confectioner". She was an agent for Marsh and Baxter's pork pies and sausages, and also sold ice creams. Just after the Second World War the Post Office moved to these premises.

In the 1950s a sweet shop was opened as an extension of the Post Office Stores. It was run from a small room attached to the White Lion and advertised as The Candy Shop, later changing its name to the Little Tuck Shop.

For a while there was a lean-to building next to the Post Office, in the present exit of the White Lion car park. This was a lock up shop, initially as a butcher's shop by Cornelius Thomas Eborall, whose shop had been next to the Ring of Bells. He was there from 1912 to 1924 and from 1924 to 1932 it was a fruiterer's run by William Corser.

An establishment which did not rate an entry in Kelly's directories was a small house in the High Street, just above 106 and where the Elm Lodge flats are now. This house had a sign outside advertising mineral waters but no more than that is known.

STATION ROAD SHOPS

There were two shops at number one Station Road and it is believed that the they were in existence from when the terrace of houses was built. One was on the corner, now a room with windows on two adjoining sides, and the second round the side. This may have been built as a shop or a store room. From 1912 to 1914 the Parish Magazine carried an advertisement for Leonard Russell a tailor, outfitter and draper. He also a dealer in boots, shoes, glass, china, household ironmongery and fancy goods. Later on a Mrs Austin is remembered as running a millinery business in Station Road but she also ran a small grocer's shop there and sold hot tea and coffee plus sandwiches. This was convenient for people attending the cattle market as a lot of livestock were driven up Station Road from the station yard at the bottom of Marsh Lane. It

The Greengrocer's Shop on the end of the old Ring of Bells building.

is understood that the grocery and the café operated from the part of the building round the corner. When the hairdressing business began at number one it was in the front but moved to the rear when the front became a private residence.

The Women's Institute Village book produced in 1965 makes the following comment:

"The shop and café in Station Road, which served the Cattle Market held in the grounds of The Engine (where Arden Court flats are now), has remained closed for many years but is now for sale with its living accommodation and may be re-opened as a hairdressing salon".

Before the hairdresser's moved to the rear the shop is remembered as a greengrocer's shop originally run by a Mr Shotton who was followed by a Mr Standley. He was the father of Chris Standley who later on ran a greengrocer's shop in Bell Vue Terrace on the side of the Old Ring of Bells building.

Between 1912 and 1922 the Parish Magazine lists W. J. Shirley having a cycle shop Station Road. He was an official repairer to the Automobile Cyclists Union and would build cycles to order from 4 to 12 guineas. The business had a branch in Meriden and eventually transferred there. The address of this business is not given but it is assumed that it was from number one.

The hardware store in Fentham Road where the shops are now.

The shops in Fentham Road just after they were built. Note that they are only two storeys.

FENTHAM ROAD SHOPS

The Fentham Road shops were built on the site of a wooden building which was a hardware store. This shop is first advertised in 1921 as Hampton Hardware Co. located in the Old Boys' School with W. A. Beamish as the proprietor. At that time they were separate from Hurst and Beamish, builders and contractors, who were, advertising as having been established for half-a-century. The wooden building in Fentham Road was demolished in the late fifties and the block of three shops in Fentham Road were opened in 1960. Initially they were two stories high.

At the time the hut was demolished it was run by Hurst and Beamish (later Hampton and Sheldon) who then occupied the shop on the right. It was then taken over by J. W. Hadley before closing in the late 1980s. Mr Hadley had taken over the electrician's business run by Mr Gibbs when he died. It had been run from an old coal merchant's shed on the railway bridge (the Meriden Road side of the station). This shop became a dress shop before becoming a print shop which lasted until very recently.

The left-hand shop has always been a chemist, but run by different people. The middle shop, now a hairdressing salon was initially a grocer's shop called the Fentham Stores. It was a mini supermarket and from 1968 to the end of 1972 and was advertised as the Fentham "V.G." Stores by John and Margaret Beach, and later, the Fentham Stores by Mr & Mrs L. H. Owen, then by D. G. & C. Roe. The last advert for the grocery business was in January 1988.

OTHER BUSINESSES IN HAMPTON

As well as the shops in Hampton there were a number of other small ventures.

There were the various refreshment rooms. These were popular in Hampton as the village attracted a large number of visitors coming for the day by train or cycling, as is seen by the adverts for tea rooms at Station Farm, run by Mrs Cox.

In Marsh Lane, the Nook (one of the cottages in Crockett's Yard) was, because of the sign

The Marsh Lane Tearooms in the 1930s.

The Station Farm Tearooms. The writing on the building says "Teas and refreshments, large and small parties catered for".

painted on the wall, known by local residents as "Teas with Hovis". The use of this cottage as refreshment rooms is first noted in the Kelly's Directory of 1896, the proprietor listed as William James Vaughan. He continues to be listed until 1928. In 1932 the refreshment room are listed as being operated by Mrs Harold Lyons who carried on until the last Kelly's directory of 1940. She is remembered by many people and her daughter-in-law still lives in the village.

The Station Farm tea rooms are known to have operated between 1912 and 1924. As well as listing Mrs Cox at Station Farm there is also an entry for S. E. Cox & Co., building and road contractors, builders merchants, plumbers, house decorators & undertakers. Initially the address was Hampton but later on they included the fact that they were also in Earlsdon, Coventry.

John Jackson, who was running a carrier's business, is listed in Kelly's Directory as having a garage in the village from 1921. This was the forerunner of the Ring of Bells garage, started in a building further up the road from its present site, where the barn cottages are now. As well as being a garage the business also generated the first electricity supply for the village.

The Ring Of Bells Garage started next to The Ring Of Bells public House.

The Ring Of Bells Garage in the late 1950s. The Post Office had been in the left hand side of the building in the 1930s.

In the early 1880s three brothers called Blackwell were looking for suitable premises to set up their businesses. Wyckham as a timber merchant, Harry as a coal merchant and Frank as a corn miller. At this stage the Stonebridge railway was not really a going concern. The extensive sidings, the Station Master's, the Branch Manager's houses and also the engine service building, all on 2.5 acres of land, were available for any other industrial use. Wyckham Blackwell began trading in home grown timber, with one circular saw, a handful of men from the village and a substantial volume of timber within ten miles on local estates. Wyckham Blackwell moved into the former managers house, now known as Vale House, and his next investment was a team of horses to pull the timber into the yard from outlying locations. He expanded into a number of different woodworking businesses. An advertisement in the Birmingham Daily Mail of 1902 sees him seeking carpenters experienced in rustic woodwork, chairs etc. Other activities have included making pews, fencing and Timberlines, a D.I.Y. shop. At the moment their main business is the construction of roof trusses for the house building industry.

Hampton had its own bank, albeit a sub-branch of a Knowle bank. It is first recorded in the Kelly's directory of 1904 as being a sub-office of the London City and Midland Bank Limited whose manager was A. Ashton Smith and was open on Mondays and Fridays. It was not until 1916 that the entry refers to the opening hours which were given as 11am until 3pm. In 1921 the name has changed to London Joint City and Midland Bank Limited and the opening hours have changed to 11am to 2pm. By 1914 it had changed its name to Midland Bank Limited but the hours and the manager were still the same. By 1928 the manager had changed to C. T. Clarke, it was open every day and the opening hours were 11am to 2.30pm. By 1936 it also opened on Saturday mornings from 10.30 to 11.30. It closed its doors after the Second World War.

The electric telegraph was invented in 1837. This device was taken up initially by the railway companies but slowly a national and international system was set up. In 1870 the operation of telegraphs was nationalised and became part of the Post Office. By the mid 1880s 39 million telegrams were being sent and Hampton Post Office, like many others handled a significant number of telegrams. A memory of this time was that of Mrs King who recalled "I left school at 14 and went to the Post Office as Telegraph Clerk to Mr Thompson, the old Postmaster: there I have been ever since, and for five years I was working from 8am to 8pm and only had one half day out and that had to be confirmed to Solihull. There was no one else in the village who could do the telegraphing". It is probable that it was this telegraphing that was behind the

The Midland Bank at Number 9 High Street.

request from Sir Frederick Peel to take the Post Office out of the general store on the site of the present corner shop and install it in the building now known as the Old Post Office.

In 1876 the telephone was invented, but at first the Post Office did not seemed interested in this new invention and so a private company was established called The National Telephone Company (NTC). In 1878 the first telephone exchange in the City of London was built in 1879. The telephone came to Hampton when the NTC set up an exchange in 5 Belle Vue Terrace in November 1907. The premises were leased by them at an annual cost of £14 6s 0d. The NTC was finally nationalised on January 1st 1912 and the telephone exchanges became the responsibility of the Postmaster General. The exchange in Belle Vue Terrace consisted of a switchboard in the front room with the equipment going in the corner under the stairs.

It should be noted that when the village had both telegraphs and telephones they operated on separate lines. Memories of the switchboard operators in Belle

This photograph, of unknown date, shows the postmen who served the village in the garden behind the Old Post Office. The wall is attached to The Cottage and the lane to the Fentham Hall is just behind them.

Vue Terrace say that during the day, from 8.30am until 10pm there were operators on duty but that there was a caretaker who looked after the exchange during the night. Apparently in the 1940s when the village doctor was Dr Christal he used to tell the exchange when he was going out on his rounds to save people being upset when there was no reply. The telephone exchange stayed in Belle Vue Terrace until 1964. Records show that in 1963 the exchange was a central battery signalling exchange with 124 business subscribers and 340 residential connections. In 1964 the exchange is listed as an Automatic non-director type system and subscribers to the system could now access the speaking clock directly, could obtain the emergency services by dialling "999" and could dial trunk calls. This new exchange was situated at the existing site in Shadow Brook Lane.

A post Second World War photo of the Cattle market.

A fledging motor company called Crowdy Limited operated in Kings Heath but, like a number of such companies, called in a receiver in 1912 and the company was bought and new directors installed. They were Lewis Radmore (Chairman) and William Miller (Secretary). It is not known where Lewis Radmore lived in Hampton but he was a noted village resident who was unfortunately killed in the first World War and he is recorded on the village War Memorial although he came from Devon. He has a trophy named after him at the North Warwickshire Golf Club. William Miller lived at a house called Wallaford in the Meriden Road (27). The new company was called Hampton Engineering and had apparently been working on motorcycles and cyclecars for at least a year under the direction of a William Paddan. William Paddan decided he could build a better car himself, and constructed a prototype 12/16 hp. in 1911. Production began in 1912 at Lifford Mills, Kings Norton, Birmingham.

Cars were assembled from imported parts including engines by Chapuis-Dornier of Paris but only a few were made before the project was killed by World War I. A 500cc motorcycle was also offered but this didn't reappear when peace returned.

After the War the company restarted in 1919 in part of an old ironworks in Dudbridge, near Stroud, Gloucestershire. The company staggered on from one crisis to another until finally ceasing to exist in 1933. The feeling is that only about 1,000 cars were made and only five cars still exist.

A business which was both old established and had a significant effect on Hampton was the Cattle Market which was where the Arden Court flats are now. The auctioneer between the wars was a Mr Whittindale who lived in The Cottage at the top of Marsh Lane.

HAMPTON-IN-ARDEN
CHRISTMAS FAT

STOCK SALE,

Tuesday, Dec. 16th, 1879,
COMPRISING

40 Ripe Fat OXEN
HEIFERS & COWS, of Grand Quality,
1 RIPE FAT BULL,
50 Ripe Fat SHEEP
CHIEFLY WETHERS,
16 Fat and Porket Pigs, &c.

The Sale comprises entries from some of the best feeders in the district, viz., James Darlington, Esq., Meriden Hall, the Right Hon. Sir. F Peel, Wm. Tibbitts, Esq., Messrs. Currall and Lewis, T. Whitehouse, W. Whitehouse, Pearman, West, Lidgate, Ward, Frost, Miss Dawes, and others.

WHITTINDALE & POTTER, Auctioneers.

Sale Ground back of the Engine Inn,
Sale at 1-30
Trains leave Coventry at 12-45, and New Street, Birmingham, at 1-10.

CATTLE TRUCKS AT THE RAILWAY STATION.

Iliffe and Son, Machine Printers, Coventry.

A handbill advertising a Christmas Fat Stock Sale.

CHAPTER ELEVEN

Hampton in Wartime

THE FIRST WORLD WAR

The First World War had a significant effect on Hampton. Not only did the newly built Fentham Hall and the attached Fentham Institute become a Red Cross Hospital but the war produced a number of changes in the social life of the village. The schoolchildren gathered various wild products to help the war effort. In 1917 the cattle market ceased to be an auction. All livestock was purchased by the Ministry of Food. The stock was graded by a farmer, a butcher and the auctioneer, now called a Certifying Officer, who acted as an arbitrator. A deduction from the price paid for a beast was paid to the auctioneer in lieu of commission. Local butchers had to attend their local market and draw lots for the cattle and if there was not enough weight to justify their customers' coupons they had a pig or sheep to make up for it.

However the biggest effect of the war was the disappearance of all the young men. At least 42 men from the village are known to have joined the forces and 23 of these lost their lives, a number of these coming from the same family. The number of deaths increased as the war continued and details are given below.

1915

Sidney Cockaigne, Company Sergeant Major, King's Royal Rifles, died 17th May, buried in the Bethune Town Cemetery in France (he came from Catherine de Barnes).

Hubert Draper, Private, Oxford and Buckinghamshire Light Infantry, died 15th September in India after being invalided there from the Persian Gulf.

1916

Gerald Dutton, Second Lieutenant, South Staffordshire Regiment, died 5th May, buried in St Peter Churchyard in Jersey.

Lewis Radmore, Flight Sub-Lieutenant, Royal Naval Air Service, died 6th September, buried in Hampton churchyard. He came from Thorveton in Devon.

William Gascoigne, no details can be found. His death is recorded in the Church Chronicle of January 1917.

1917

Walter Woodward, Private, 11th Battalion, Royal Warwickshire Regiment, killed in action in France on 22nd February 1917, commemorated on the Loos Memorial in France.

George Cliffe Jenkins, Second Lieutenant, York and Lancaster Regiment, died 3rd May, commemorated on the Arras Memorial in France.

Ralph Baker, Gunner, Royal Artillery, died 18th May, buried in the Cambrai East Military Cemetery in France.

Ernest Bailey, Sapper, Royal Engineers, died 8th July, buried in the Coxyde Military Cemetery, Koksijde in Belgium.

Percy Shirley, Corporal, 10th Battalion, Royal Warwickshire Regiment, died 20th September, commemorated on the Tyne Cot Memorial in Belgium.

1918

Leslie Hill, Able Seaman, Royal Navy Volunteer Reserve, died 19th February, commemorated on the Plymouth Naval Memorial.

Alfred Borley, Corporal, Railway Operating Company, Royal Engineers, died from pneumonia 15th May, buried in the Longuenesse (St Omer) Souvenir Cemetery in France.

Percy Poole, Private, 281st Company, Machine Gun Corps, died 12 October, commemorated on the Kirkee 1915-1918 Memorial, India.

Reginald Blamire, Private, 1st Battalion, Royal Warwickshire Regiment, died 19th November, buried in the Preseau Communal Cemetery Extension in France.

Cornelius Cull, Private, 2nd Battalion, Royal Warwickshire Regiment, died 24th November, commemorated at the Cologne Southern Cemetery in Germany (he came from Catherine de Barnes).

Harry Blizzard, Pioneer, 314th Road Construction Company, Royal Engineers, died 1st December, buried in Maubeuge (Sous-le-bois) Cemetery in France.

Edgar King, Leading Seaman, HMS St. Vincent, died 20 December, buried in the Portsmouth (Kingston) Cemetery.

In addition to the above we can find no further details of the following men.

John Henderson

Colin James Jones

Charles Victor Jones, but believed to have served in the Royal Warwickshire Regiment,

Thomas Pargeter Jones, John Savage and William Savage.

The death of a William Mason is recorded in the Church Chronicle of March 1917 but his name is on the Barston War Memorial.

The following men are known to have served in the Armed Forces.

Henry Austin, seriously wounded.

Ralph Baker, Prisoner of War in Germany.

Arthur Berwick, wounded.

Harvey Burrill, wounded.

William Corser, Private, King's Royal Rifles, Prisoner of War in Germany.

Harry Draper, Private, Royal Warwickshire Regiment, reported missing.

Hugh Draper, Private, Home Defence Force.

Louis Draper, Private, West Yorkshire Regiment.

Tom Draper, Private, Kings Royal Rifles, gassed and wounded in 1915, reported missing in 1918.

Noel Draper, Drummer, Worcestershire Regiment.

Sidney Homer, Guardsman, Coldstream Guards, by 1915 he had been wounded three times and had been awarded the Distinguished Conduct Medal for conspicuous bravery in action.

Harvey King, Private, 2nd Canadian Contingent.

Fred Knight, Corporal, Queen's Own West Surry Regiment, and was awarded the Military Medal for distinguished conduct in France.

Bert Large, wounded.

Fred Mason, wounded.

Norrie, Major, wounded, awarded the Distinguished Service Order for gallant service in the field.

H. Nottingham, Trooper, Warwickshire Yeomanry.

Les Poole, Private, South Staffordshire Regiment.

Tom Poole, Private, 7th Battalion, Royal Warwickshire Regiment.

HAMPTON DURING THE SECOND WORLD WAR

Life in Hampton during the Second World War was a mixture of events which were specifically related to the war and those consistent with the peace time existence of the village. The first thing that happened was that a lot of wartime services were provided by volunteers. This did not just suddenly start in September 1939, the war had been expected since early 1938. A recruitment campaign was launched to speed up enrolments in national service and consisted of three daily sessions where the different schemes were outlined and volunteers enrolled. This covered not only air raid precautions but also recruits for civil

The War Memorial was dedicated by the bishop of Birmingham on 23rd July 1921. Note Burrill's bottom shop and Shepherds Row in the back ground.

nursing and the W.V.S. (Womens' Voluntary Service) looking for people to help in canteen cookery.

Another development in 1938 was the building of an Ammunition Storage Depot on the outskirts of the village. This involved diverting a public footpath and it included a small bungalow for the Superintendent of the facility (now extended and called Midfield).

By May 1939, various branches of national service were organised in the village. A.R.P. (Air Raid Precautions) courses in first aid and what to do if a gas attack occurred had been completed and thirty men and women were considered to be qualified for the work. A First Aid Point was established in the former stables of the Manor, (in what is now Manor Cottage) loaned by Mrs Rollason who lived in the Manor House. It had a dressing room and six beds where patients could be kept in comfort to await removal to more permanent quarters. There was a separate store where a comprehensive supply of surgical equipment, blankets, hot-water bottles, first–aid haversacks, two wheeled stretchers, hurricane lamps etc were kept. Facilities for heating and alternative lighting were available and there were ample supplies of hot water.

Ex-servicemen from the village line up in Belle Vue Terrace ready to march down the hill for the unveiling of the War Memorial.

One highly important duty of the A.R.P. was firefighting, and members of the A.F.S. (Auxiliary Fire Service) were trained and expected to provide adequate protection.

A survey of the village for the purpose of accommodating evacuated children was made and a Red Cross detachment was organised. There were enough volunteers to form three sections. Dr Christal, the village doctor, was the tutor and lectures in home nursing were organised by the W.I.

By January 1941 a fire-watching service had been organised by the Parish Council, a rota prepared and patrols were in operation.

During the First World War the Fentham Hall had been used as a Red Cross hospital and every one expected it to be used again for the same purpose. However it was reported in August 1939 that if a national emergency was declared, a hospital would not be established in Hampton. It had been decided to use the mental hospital in Marston Green instead, and the Hampton detachment were to help staff it. In September 1941 the local detachment of the Red Cross received a mobile canteen as a gift from American citizens. It was for use in the event of air raids and was based in Hampton and put on view at The Engine.

The W.V.S. had recruited women and trained them in canteen cookery. They first put their skills into action in December 1940. Many people from Coventry and

Birmingham who had suffered from enemy action came to Hampton to take shelter in the village. A band of Hampton women cared for some of those rendered homeless at the Fentham Hall. Working in shifts of ten they provided mid-day soup and hot drinks at night. At first 150 found shelter in the Hall but half of these were later billeted in the village where practically every house was used.

The Fentham Hall was not the only place used for evacuees. A family that came here after being bombed out in Birmingham consisting of two adults and two children, had been in their Anderson shelter and although they were not hurt their house was demolished and they did manage to rescue some furniture. They did not recall why they came to Hampton but they were brought here in a relative's van and they initially slept in the W.I. room (now the library). After a short time they were allocated a single room in the servants' quarters of the Vicarage. They cooked and ate as well as slept in that room. They were allowed to go to a house in the Meriden Road for baths.

The husband of the family was called up in 1941 and the mother heard that there were some empty servants rooms at the Manor. She asked Mrs Rollason if she could live there and received her agreement. The rooms were for the third gardener who had been called up and couldn't be replaced. In fact the Manor kept two gardeners during the war, both men who were approaching retirement age. The rooms used were on the end of the building where the Manor Office is now. Not only did the wife and two children live there but they were later joined by the grandparents who had another two rooms in the same block.

For a short time there were ten families sleeping at the Manor. At least three of the families stayed in the village for the rest of the war.

The local detachment of the Home Guard was part of the 5th Warwickshire (Solihull) Battalion. It consisted of 30 good men and true, picked from the elite of those left behind, who, for one reason or another, could not go into the forces. The detachment was initially based at Beech House, its actual H.Q. being the garage at the rear. This was chosen because of the easy access through the garden between the High Street and Fentham Road. The garage was properly equipped with pitch forks, pick handles, catapults and other defensive weapons until the men were issued with old American rifles which were packed with grease. It was the wives' job to clean them with boiling water. It then turned out that as well as being old, the rifles were not 303 calibre like the British rifle, with the result that ammunition had to be specially made for them.

Six men were on duty each night and they all took it in turns to sleep in the loft of the garage on straw palliasses. Although they all took their job very seriously, it was suspected that if Hampton were invaded they would probably all run home to see to their own families first! As the war progressed the Home Guard transferred to the old Girls' School, a more secure H.Q. As far as is known they did not encounter the enemy, although someone did report a rifle being pointed at a low flying aircraft!

The war brought a whole series of new regulations such as the black out laws. In October 1940, a resident of Meriden Road was fined £2 for an infringement of the black out. A light was showing from an unscreened bedroom window and the householder said that it was obviously an accident. In November 1940 a resident of Diddington Lane was fined £3 for a similar offence. The police said that a light caused by a hall door being occasionally opened was shining from a large landing window. The comment made was that the resident had only just taken the house and had had a curtain made and had not yet fixed it up. He said that it was not an intense beam of light.

In July 1942, a lady in The Crescent who broke the black out regulations was also fined £2. A light was shining through a skylight from a room over her garage and she thought that it must have been left on by some men who had been repairing her water system. She said she could not see the light from the house.

If you had a car then the lights on it had to be screened. In April 1940 a man from Eastcote Lane was fined 10s for driving a car with unscreened side lights. All motor vehicles had to be immobilised before being left unattended. A young man from Bellemere Road was fined in respect of his motor bike. He claimed that he had only stopped to get a packet of cigarettes and did not think that it was necessary to immobilise it when he was leaving it for so short a time. He was fined 25s.

The screening of lights on a car applied equally to what in those days were always called pedal cycles. In March 1940 a man from Old Station Road was fined 5s for cycling without a fully screened front light.

On October 17th 1942 the Warwick County News carried the Headline "Hampton Man stored Too Much Coke". There were a lot of wartime regulations and one specified the amount of fuel that you could store. It turned out that the man in question had sixteen tons of coal and coke in a barn. He was fined £77 for this offence. The company that had supplied the fuel was also fined £77 because it was not licensed to do so.

There were also cases of petty crime. In January 1941, two Hampton men were fined £10 each for receiving four stolen Army blankets.

In September 1941 two incidents were reported by the village constable. Two youths from Acocks Green were fined 10s each for flattening ten square yards of mowing grass, damage estimated at £1 and both were fined 12s 5d. Apparently

The Ammunition Storage Dump in Meriden Road. This shows the road before it was straightened.

they had been late going home and had lain down in a hayfield to sleep. The second incident concerned four men who were fined 11s 3d each for stealing mushrooms from a field where they were being grown.

In January 1940 the Old Boys Club, a hut in the school grounds later used as the school canteen, was requisitioned for use as billets for 18 men of the 81st LAA (Light Anti Aircraft) Battery of the Royal Artillery. Some of them were also based in the Old Ring of Bells, the building having ceased to be a pub in October 1938.

On October 3rd 1940 it was noted that three air raid warnings were heard and then, after heavy raids on Coventry on 15th November and on Birmingham on November 20th, about 20 children were admitted to the school following their evacuation from Coventry and Birmingham.

The children spent quite a lot of time in the shelters during the first few months but this caused problems so that by January 1941 it had been agreed to carry on with school work during air raids and only to stop if actual danger threatened. This had been approved by the majority of parents.

In April there were more air raids on Coventry and Birmingham and some high explosive bombs were dropped in the Manor grounds, probably by accident. Some incendiaries were also dropped in the village.

The Anti-Aircraft site in Old Station Road just before the road goes under the old railway line.

From then the problems of air raids seem to have faded away and as far as the children were concerned the only things related to the war seem to have been a propensity to ask them to collect things. During War Weapons Week in 1941, the school collected £1,021 on the first day and reached £1,600 by the end of the week. These were National Savings rather than donations.

But collections of money were made and the school diary notes that in May 1941 the money collected under the Red Cross penny a week scheme was forwarded to the Lord Mayor of London for a London child who had suffered in the air raids. In June a second amount collected under the scheme was sent to the Prisoners of War Fund.

In January 1942 they collected waste paper, 19 cwt in the first week. In March 1942 during Warships Week the school contribution was £15,157.

June 22nd 1942 saw the start of school meals in Hampton the Old Boys Club building having been converted into the school canteen. On that day fifty dinners were sold at a cost of 4d a head. But there were a lot of problems with the equipment and although meals continued to be provided there were times when they had to be brought in from elsewhere. But the provision of school meals was a direct result of a large number of mothers having to go out to work.

There were a large number of money raising schemes held in the village. The most significant scheme was the annual savings weeks. These started off being called War Weapons Weeks but were later given more specific names. The War Weapons Week in 1942 became Warship Week and was part of a district campaign to get people to invest in various national savings. The village was given a target to raise £8,000 for Warship Week and various events were organised to persuade people to invest. The sum invested by the end of that week was £57,061 or £43 per head of the population.

In 1943 the War Weapons Week was called Wings for Victory Week and again the village had a target, this time it was raised to £17,000. The village excelled itself and the sum collected was well over the target being £48,370. In April 1944 it became Salute the Soldier week with a target of £22,000. Again the village responded well with £34,554 being invested.

Before these national savings events were organised there were some other money raising schemes. A War Weapons Week in 1940 raised £301 7s. In 1941 a Spitfire Fund was started with £120 being raised. Clearly not on the same lines as the savings events but there were other local money raising schemes as well.

The Hampton Gymkhana, which became such a feature of later village life as the Hampton Horse Show up until the early nineteen eighties, started as a one-off event in 1944 to raise money for the Red Cross.

A Forces Comforts Fund was started in 1940 with the objective of sending articles to Hampton men in the armed forces. Later on it included women.

In August 1940 the women of Hampton had knitted 35 pairs of socks which were sent to the village men serving in the forces. At the same time a fund of £7 3s had been raised which resulted in 19 parcels containing cigarettes, magazines, chocolate and soap being sent off.

Not only were local men serving in the forces catered for but there was a group committed to giving support to locally stationed troops. A committee was formed in 1941 and the Old Boys Club (the club for old boys of the Boys' School was used as a place for the troops to relax in).

In June 1942 it was announced that help in catering for Hampton housewives would be offered by the new "Pie Scheme" to be initiated by the Women's

Institute. It was part of a Government programme for communal feeding in rural areas where women, far from shopping centres, were considered to be at a disadvantage. The W.I. decided to open a local Pie Centre as soon as the necessary permits had been received from the Food Office.

In August 1942 the Pie Scheme came into operation. Members attended each Thursday for the distribution of pies. Apparently 238 pies were distributed on the first occasion but they expected the number to increase as more people became aware of the scheme. The pies were cooked in the W.I. Room to begin with but later on were cooked in the butcher's shop. By July 1943 the number of pies sold every week had increased to 300.

As regards the fruit preservation scheme it seemed to have a mixed success. In October 1941 the Fruit Preservation Centre was closed due to lack of fruit. But it reopened as fruit became available again and a report in June 1942 states that the W.I. had made 37 pounds of Gooseberry Jam.

Hampton was concerned that an influx of people, both troops and evacuees, would have an effect on normal life in the village. But it all proved groundless and the village welcomed both troops and evacuees with open arms. At least one local girl married a G.I.

As the first act of welcome a committee was formed at the instigation of the British Legion to provide welfare for troops stationed locally.

The Ammunition Dump had been built in the summer of 1939 and was initially the responsibility of the Royal Engineers although it was later run by the Pioneer Corps. The site was selected as providing easy access by road to the anti aircraft batteries protecting Birmingham and Coventry.

The function of the Dump was to supply ammunition to all large guns in the area as and when needed. Quite a few men and lorries were based there. When an air raid warning was sounded the doors of the bunkers would open and out would come the lorries laden with ammunition, ready to be sent to the nearest gun emplacement which might need topping up. Inspection of the site shows that it is quite big and that it is possible that a lot of unreported activities went on there. One of the anti-aircraft batteries was based alongside the old railway line just off Old Station Road.

In 1944 U.S. troops arrived and many of them had to be billeted in the village. The billeting order stated that they must be provided with breakfast, a hot dinner, tea and supper on each day and laid down how much meat, etc must be included in the meal. For providing this the householder was paid 1s a day.

A copy of the billeting order dated 22nd April 1944 to Mrs Mary Jordan stated that she was required to find billets for 4 U.S. soldiers. A covering note said that she would receive a payment of £1 8s 0d for the period 25/5/44 to 7/6/44.

The Jordans only had two soldiers in the end. They were a Corporal Shockey and Pfc. (Private First Class) Frank Clarke. They were part of the 3rd Platoon of the 54th Field Hospital.

The unit itself was based at Fentham Hall and as well as using the Hall had two ridge tents in what is now the Car Park. There were apparently about 100 people in the Field Hospital including some female nurses. Many of them were billeted locally including six in one of the big semi-detached houses at the beginning of Diddington Lane. The nurses were billeted at the Manor.

Whilst he was here Pfc. Frank Clarke celebrated his twenty-first birthday party and stood drinks in the White Lion to celebrate. American tin helmets have a plastic insert and Frank Jones put all his small change in his and then put it on the counter of the White Lion saying that drinks were on him until the money ran out.

In January 1940 we find that the Parish Magazine giving details of a social event adds the line "Please bring your gas mask".

Life in Hampton, although typical of other villages was severely disrupted during the war years. Family life altered. The majority of the younger men went away to join the forces and some of those who stayed behind joined the Home Guard or became A.R.P. wardens which meant that after working all day they then worked all night as well. Women who did not have a child under 8 years old, were ordered to go to work to do the jobs that the men had done. The 8.15 train from Hampton to Birmingham was always full of women going to work on offices, factories etc.

A lot of outsiders came to Hampton during those years. As well as the evacuees and the soldiers there were the girls of the Women's Land Army and a small sub-group of the Land Army called the Women's Timber Corps who were used by Wyckham Blackwell both in the woods and in the sawmills.

As Denis Butler mentions in his book on Wyckham Blackwell timber was an important commodity during the war and the company supplied timber for both the wing frame sections of mosquitoes as well as pit props, railway sleepers and other essential items for the war effort. He also mentions other problems caused to nearly all firms during the war which were the regulations, in his case the licensing of all timber production. Regulations became a way of life during the war as did finding ways round them.

As the war was coming to a close in 1944/5 there were long and heated debates about the form of war memorial to be provided.

One suggestion was the provision of 24 houses for disabled ex-servicemen, war widows and their families. Later on Meriden Rural District Council wanted all its villages to build community centres to be war memorials. Hampton rejected both ideas. The village memorial was a refurbishment of the Fentham Hall to which both the Fentham Trust and the villagers contributed.

As in the previous war a large number of Hampton men served in the forces. The Church and Village Chronicle records 86 men and 3 women. Unlike the First World War there was not the great loss of life and only one name was added to the War Memorial, Sergeant John Mallaber R.A.F., serving as an air gunner. In addition Sergeant William Butler R.A.F., who had lived in the village, died and is recorded on the Malta Memorial.

CHAPTER TWELVE

Village Organisations

GARDEN CLUB

Aconsiderable number of reports have appeared over the years in the parish magazine of village horticultural activities. In May 1870, an article was printed, offering prizes of ten shillings, seven shillings and four shillings for the three neatest, and best cultivated large gardens, and the same amount for small gardens.

In August of this year an advertisement appeared stating that the 'Cottagers Garden Society, would be holding their second Horticultural Show in that month. A later report of this 'Annual Show of Flowers and Fruit' stated that various specimens of garden produce were arranged in a spacious tent erected in the grounds of the Rt. Hon. Sir Frederick Peel, decorated with evergreens and adorned with choice flowers. The products exhibited also included a wide variety of vegetables grown in the member's gardens and devices formed of grasses and wild flowers by the local children.

Forty prizes of one to two shillings were given across the range of produce. The publication of the balance sheet showed a total cost of £29 18s 4d. £9 9s 0d was paid to the Band, and 12s to the attending Police Officers.

Many other gardening articles were printed over the years, essays on Cottage Gardening, and Gardeners Calendar of Operations, together with adverts for the sale of garden produce.

An article for the forthcoming 'Cottagers Garden Inspection' for the three prizes, ended with a delightful little comment,

"There are few who do not value, to a greater or less degree, the piece of ground which they may call their own, and which affords to the man of quiet habits a constant source of praiseworthy gratification". The Cottagers Garden Society appears to be a group of village enthusiasts, tending their own gardens. There are no records of garden club meetings, as we have today, only the annual Village Horticultural and Flower Show, always held in The Manor grounds. The admission fee was one shilling, children free and 'Labourers' after 4pm paid 3d. Reports of this event appeared regularly until 1883 and always contained a detailed list of categories and prize winners.

On other occasions the Garden Society was involved in flower shows and garden fetes held for the benefit of church related charities, with an evening dance in the marquee, always ending at 8pm with the National Anthem. One such Fete, held in grand style, in the vicarage garden, included a display of needlework from the Kensington School of Art, lawn tennis, archery, demonstrations by the Warwickshire Bee Keeping Association and a performance of Haydn's Toy Symphony.

The annual garden fetes and flower shows remained popular events throughout the years, and some were run on a grand style. On Saturday August 11th 1917 it was announced that a Garden Sale was to be held between 3pm and 7pm, in the grounds of Thorpe Grange, by kind permission of Mr & Mrs Neville Edwards Tidy. There would be various stalls and competitions, together with tea and refreshments. The net proceeds from this event was £84 10s 5d. Of this £42 12s 2d was given to the Diocesan Treasury, £10 10s 0d to the cause of Foreign Missions and the remainder placed in the Churchwarden's deposit account for future garden events. Unfortunately Thorpe Grange cannot be traced. There are no records of such a house near the centre of the village, but there are thoughts that it was in the area of the Packhorse bridge and Bradnocks Marsh.

In July 1924, a Garden Fete and Rose Show, a new title and activity in the gardeners calendar, was held with twenty-five stalls and old style fairground activities, coconut shies, balloon races, aunt sally, ankle competitions and the inevitable character reading from a 'Gypsy Rose Lee'. American Tea was served, this seemed to be very popular and was often served at other events in the village during this period. Sales on the Fancy, the Hardware, the Produce Stalls, and Mrs Jacques' 'Well Worth' stall produced a total amount of £91 0s 6d on that afternoon. The sale of ice cream fetched £19 2s 6d and the main event, the Rose Show brought in £32 17s 6d. Total receipts for the afternoons activities amounted to £256 7s 1d. The event was obviously well attended, and by villagers it appears, who were willing to dig deeply into their pockets and purses.

A members' contribution card for the Ring of Bells Horticultural Society, dated 1937 and signed by the secretary, Mr Corser, stated: The rules are very simple, Entrance Fee 1s, weekly contribution 6d. Any member being more than two months in arrears will be excluded. This is the first time that we see a gardening group meeting on a regular basis, possibly brought about by a group of enthusiasts needing some alcoholic beverage after their hard labours.

Apart from the usual church fetes there are few reports of gardening activities until 1976, when Mr Charles Keatley announced that 'Le Club Jardin' would meet on the first Tuesday in every month in preparation for the coming Flower

Festival. In 1984 a Gardening Class was run in conjunction with the Hampton Community Crafts, held in the Fentham Annexe.

Eight years later, on Wednesday, October 3rd 1984 a gardening class, run in association with the Hampton Community Crafts met in the Fentham Annexe, and a decision was made to organise themselves into a Garden Society. Martin Poole was elected Chairman and John Trumper as Secretary and Treasurer. The purpose of the society was - To meet indoors in the colder months and outdoors in the warmer months. Discussions will take place amongst the members, including related jobs for the month. Experts will be invited to give talks, and visits organised to other gardens. It was around this time that Martin Poole re-named the garden club as The Hampton Garden Society, together with the motto, G.G.D.S.M. (Good Gardeners Don't Spend Money).

A joining fee of £2, plus 50p per meeting was proposed, and the first meeting took place in the Fentham Annexe on November 7th 1984. In addition to the gardening activities, wine making and pickling was also covered. Martin was renowned for his appreciation of alcoholic beverages. This raises a possible question for the present committee of the Hampton-in-Arden Garden Club, should this activity be revived?

Apart from this additional activity there has been very little change, the details of the Garden Club's activities and events show a similar pattern over the years. Even as early as 1985, a young Tristan Thacker gave a talk titled, Down The Garden Path, and he has continued to lead us down this way ever since. By 1987, there were changes to the organisation, there was a general feeling that a formal committee should be established to run the club's activities. Robin Lawrence was elected as the first Chairman, Janice Thorpe as Secretary, Stan Bamber as Treasurer, and committee members Audrey Phillips and Jean Shepherd. The meeting venue was then changed to the Church Hall.

A set pattern began to emerge in the Garden Club calendar. A club Bulb Competition was established in April for the Madge Bamber Plate. In May, there was for many years a trip to the Malvern Spring Show. In the summer months there was an organised Open Garden Weekend, hosted by members, the club evening Garden Party, with Strawberries and Fizz, and the Club Produce Show of flowers, fruit and vegetables judged by Tristan Thacker. October produced a very short Annual General Meeting and to end the year a Christmas Party was organised in December with a garden quiz, table decoration competitions, carols, mince pies and hot punch.

In the monthly meetings members were entertained with talks and demonstrations from experts on a wide variety of garden related subjects.

Daytime and evening outings were organised to formal gardens and garden centres always with a very sociable meal at a local hostelry. In 1999 the garden club committee organised a four-day holiday to visit a selection of gardens in Kent. This event was such a success that it was continued with a second trip in 2002 to Hampshire and Dorset and a third in 2005 to Norfolk.

There is little doubt about the popularity of this village garden club, shown by the number of members that crowd the Church Hall each month. The dedication and hard work carried out by the committee continues to earn much appreciation by the members, and has made Hampton the envy of many other gardening clubs in the area.

The Hampton Flower Show Prize List printed in the Chronicle in September 1870

			s	d	£	s	d
Jones. John	1st prize	Three cabbages	2	0			
	"	Six spring onions	2	0			
	"	Six winter onions	2	0			
	3rd prize	Six carrots	1	0			
	"	Six turnips	1	0			
	"	Shallots	1	0	9	0	
Price. John	3rd prize	Three cabbages	1	0			
	"	Twenty four peas (Pods)	1	0			
	2nd prize	Garden Herbs	1	6			
	"	Fruit (four sorts)	2	0	5	6	
Tustin. Charlotte	Extra	Fruit (Single dish of)	1	6	1	6	
Edwards. Edwin	2nd prize	Six parsnips	1	6			
	"	Six carrots	1	6			
	Extra	Six spring onions	2	0			
	3rd prize	Celery (Three sticks of)	1	0			
	1st prize	Three vegetable marrows	2	0	8	0	
Draper. Joseph	3rd prize	Nosegay	1	0	1	0	
Taylor. Richard	1st prize	Best Small Garden	10	0			
	3rd prize	Four useful vegetables	1	0			
	2nd prize	Twenty four peas (Pods)	1	6			
	1st prize	Garden Herbs	2	0			
	2nd prize	Three window plants	2	0			
	"	Cut flowers (Collection of)	1	6	18	0	
Draper. Edward	3rd prize	Best Large Garden	4	0			

			s	d	£	s	d
	"	Eight useful vegetables	2	0			
	"	Six parsnips	1	0			
	"	Twenty four	1	0		8	0
		(Dwarf French Beans)					
Mann. Henry	2nd prize	Twenty four scarlet runners	1	6			
	"	Rhubarb	1	6			
	3rd prize	Garden Herbs	1	0		4	0
Blackwell. Andrew	3rd prize	Twelve round potatoes	1	0			
	"	Twenty four scarlet runners	1	0		2	0
Smith. William	1st prize	Twelve round potatoes	2	0		2	0
Smith. Charles	1st prize	Best Large Garden	10	0			
	3rd prize	Twelve kidney potatoes	1	0			
	1st prize	Twelve flat or fluke shape	2	0			
	"	Twenty four peas (Pods)	2	0			
	2nd prize	Six winter onions	1	6			
	1st prize	Six parsnips	2	0			
	"	Six carrots	2	0			
	2nd prize	Celery (three sticks of)	1	6			
	1st prize	Six turnips	2	0			
	"	Shallots	2	0			
	Extra	Cucumber	1	0	1	7	0
Francis. William	Special	Model garden	3	0		3	0

Children's Designs of Wild Flowers

				s	d
Blood. George	1st prize			3	0
Blick. Benjamin	2nd prize			2	0
Ashfield. Annie	3rd prize			1	0

May Pole Design

		s	d
A. M. Smith, A. Hancock and H. Smith. (Prize given by a Lady)		5	0

It is interesting to see the costs incurred from the Statement of Accounts presented, particularly the payment made to the Police.

	£	s	d		£	s	d
Balance from last year	13	8	10	Price list	9	1	9
Members tickets		13	6	Paid for Tent	3	10	0

	£	s	d			£	s	d
Received from visitors	26	4	3	Paid for Band		9	9	0
Donations	1	2	6	Paid for Table covers			14	0
Interest on deposit		6	1	Paid for Tables & Fixing		1	15	0
				Paid for Police Officers			12	0
				Paid for Ticket Collectors			6	0
				Paid for Postages & Incidental Expenses			16	3
				Paid for Allowance to Secretary			10	0
				Paid for Printing Account		3	3	6
						29	18	4
				Balance in Treasurers Hand		11	16	10
Rev. T. J. Morris. Chairman	41	15	2			41	15	2

MEN'S CLUBS

In 1869 a report appeared in one of the first editions of the Hampton-in-Arden Parish Magazine showing concern by the Vicar and Sir Frederick Peel, for the level of education and the social behaviour in the village. With considerable financial help from local residents and grants from two Book Societies the Hampton-in-Arden Parochial Lending Library was opened in the Girls Schoolroom.

Strict rules were established stating – 'That every member subscribing 1s per annum (to be paid in advance) be entitled to receive from the library, one book of religious and one of a useful and entertaining character. This Parochial Library was reported in the chronicle for the next seventeen years and obviously enjoyed by a certain level of village society.

This was repeated in the Chronicle, once again in 1877, when the Reverend Theodore Morris, the vicar of Hampton at that time, and Sir Frederick Peel stressed their concern at the increase in young male troublemakers in the village. Although there was a considerable amount of social activity in the village at this time, lectures, plays and musical evenings, mostly in the Girls' School, this was a little too sophisticated for some of the young farm labourers. The only other option of course was the village pub.

An article in the 1877, October issue of the village chronicle stated the intention to open a 'Coffee and Reading Room' for men, from Monday to

Saturday between 6.30pm and 10pm during the winter months, and supplied with newspapers and magazines. There would also be a Recreation Room with provision for games of draughts, bagatelle, dominoes and other similar amusements. Membership was limited to men above the age of sixteen on payment of a small weekly sum, at first considered to be about 1 pence, and later set at 1d per night or 3d per month. The decoration and furnishing of the Rooms, the location of which was never disclosed, was paid for by donations from Sir Frederick and a few other residents of the village.

In the November issue of the magazine, it was reported that the rooms were *"very snug and comfortable and at about seven o'clock thirty new members sat down to an excellent tea followed by a reading of the rules and the urging of all those young men to consider the importance, of rightly employing their leisure hours"*. By December, it was reported that the numbers had increased to fifty and that Mrs Bally had presented a 'Handsome Clock,' for the convenience of the members.

In October 1883, the club was re-named The Hampton-in-Arden Mutual Improvement Society, a rather grand title for a Working Men's Club. The Reverend Morris was named as the first president. A chronicle report stated that coffee and buns would be supplied at a low cost, and that on alternate Saturday meetings there would be a lecture or reading followed by a discussion.

By late 1884, the name had reverted to the original Reading and Recreation Rooms. For a number of years it had been considered that a permanent home was needed for the men of the village - 'for Social Intercourse and Instructive Evenings'. A number of local residents, headed by Sir Frederick Peel, donated money to the cause, which enabled a newly formed committee to rent the three-roomed house lately occupied by Mr Garlick, who was now living at, and running the grocery business at the corner shop. A brief report by the vicar stated that it was very convenient as it was next door to the vicarage. This being the old vicarage site next to the White Lion, this house would be at the top of the first block of cottages, number 24, High Street.

A balance sheet in January 1888 shows donations of £16 16s 7d from thirty two residents and 10s given by the servants of the Manor. The receipts from sales of coffee and biscuits over the winter period of 1887 and 1888 was £17 3s 5d.

In the winter of 1889, the club was being run entirely from village donations and the subscription charge had been dropped. The house was completely re-decorated and a new rule was laid down, that those who used it 'Shall be of the sterner sex and that their conduct and general behaviour shall be seemly and decorous'. Does this suggest that conduct in the past was not always of a high standard.

It appears that the activities of the Men's Club had ceased by 1908, in November of that year, a group of male parishioners met in the Boys' Schoolroom and discussed the opening of a Recreation Club for men.

It was eventually opened, possibly in the schoolroom, with meetings every Wednesday evening in the winter months for men over seventeen at 1s per session. This was still a church bonded activity and presided over by the vicar. In April 1910, the Birmingham News contained reports of whist, cribbage and air gun matches involving the Men's Social Club, in the Bulls Head, Meriden, which were all won by Hampton.

By the beginning of the First World War, these Reading and Recreation Room activities appear to have ceased. In 1913 the Fentham Trust purchased a house originally called The Beeches and with much interior alteration, turned it into a new social centre for the men of the village. Details of which can be found, in this book, under the heading of 'Fentham Club and Hall'.

In the Summer of 1987, another 'Mens Club' was formed, with an initial membership of nineteen men from the village, but this was different! These were not working men in need of social care and educational enhancement, they were a group of retired 'gentlemen' desirous of social companionship. The meetings were held each month in the Church Hall with an organised speaker, mixed with the occasional trip out to a local pub for lunch. In 1991, the club had an invitation from John Moffatt, the landlord of the White Lion, to hold its meetings in the back room of the pub. At about the same time it officially became a Probus Club, part of the organisation established, 'to provide facilities for retired professional and business men to meet others in similar circumstances'. Over the next few years the activities of the club were extended, to include outings and visits to places of interest, including an annual Ladies Day trip. A Probus Plodders group was formed, possibly for the exercise they provided, or more likely for the social pub lunch that was included at the half-way point. By the late 1990s, the membership had increased to over sixty, with some prospective members waiting for up to two years to join. The club's meetings and other activities were well attended, with the added attraction of a Christmas lunch held in the back room of the White Lion.

In 2004, this room had been re-furnished by the new owner and was neither large enough nor suitable for Probus meetings, and so the move was made back to the Church Hall. The membership is still high and sporting activities have been added, golf and croquet tournaments, and an annual bowls challenges against the Women's Institute for the coveted Rolling Pin prize. In an ageing society new, younger retired members are always required to help maintain the enthusiasm and energy that this club has always enjoyed.

FENTHAM CLUB AND HALL

The large white-faced building and the even larger extension on the right hand side, visible through its entrance at the junction of Marsh Lane and Fentham Road, has had a complex history of ownership and uses. Originally a private house named The Beeches, it became the Fentham Institute, a men's club, in 1919, and then re-named the Fentham Club, when the ladies were admitted, until its closure in 2003. It re-opened as a mixture of club bar and restaurant, called The Grange, which failed to attract many customers and after much redecorating finally opened again in October 2005 as an upmarket restaurant, and returned to its original name The Beeches.

The house was built, sometime in the 1830s by Louisa Moore, the widowed daughter of William Eborall of Balsall, and the last remaining member of the Eborall family. William, who died in 1821 is buried in the Altar Tomb outside the vestry door of Hampton church, alongside his five year old son Henry. Louisa's two sisters, Susannah and Caroline are buried together with their mother in the north aisle of the church. The Eborall family had maintained close connections with the church for many years, the name board of Hampton vicars hung on the south wall of the church shows a Robert Eyberhale, reputed to be an early spelling of Eborall, serving as the vicar of Hampton in 1391.

In about 1840 Louisa married Edmund Simonds, a widower, who had recently moved to Hampton from Liverpool where he had been an active member of the Dr Raffles' Congregational Church. He, his son Robert and George Simonds, a confectioner from Atherstone, were amongst the sixteen trustees and founders, who built the Hampton Congregational Church in Butchers Road in 1838.

Edmund died two years after Louisa in December 1856, aged 75, and even though a non-conformist he was allowed to be buried with her in the north aisle of the Parish Church next to her two sisters.

Two children from his previous marriage remained in the village. His daughter, whose married name was Sophia Guest Atkin, lived at Rose Cottage next to The Beeches, and his son Robert at a house called The Laurels in Fentham Road, close to the Congregational Church.

In the late 1800s two very detailed reports were printed in the Church Chronicle, of the marriage of the two daughters of Mr Robert King, a Birmingham Galvanised Iron Merchant. In April 1873, Miss Harriet 'Hattie' King was married to the Reverend Alfred William Horton, referred to as a Clerk in Order. The reception was held in the drawing room of The Beeches and in a marquee in the garden. In 1883, her sister married Charles Arthur Horton –

Two views taken of the front and rear gardens of The Beeches. The front, now the car park entrance from Marsh Lane, taken in the late 1800s, and the rear garden now the Bowling Green.

'Gentleman'. Brothers maybe, or was it just a coincidence? The reception, once again held at the Beeches included an Evening Ball.

Census records relating to The Beeches show three changes of ownership, Solomon Shakespeare in the 1860s, Robert King up to the late 1880s and finally Frank Lindner up to the purchase by the Fentham Trust in 1913.

In 1907, the Charity Commissioners had produced a new scheme which affected all charities, and under the heading of 'General benefits to the Poor' it gave the George Fentham Trustees the power to make contributions towards the provision and maintenance of a Reading Room or Working Men's Club. In 1913, under this new scheme, the Trustees acquired The Beeches and began converting it for this purpose. At the same time they began building an extension, to be called the Fentham Hall, which hopefully would provide an income for the benefit of the charity. This was completed in 1914, but it would be another five years before it was eventually used for any village activities.

A year before the First World War commenced, a group of local residents, led by professional medical staff had formed The Hampton Detachment, part of a national scheme to prepare for the onslaught of war. They were trained in first aid and nursing procedures, and in August 1914 the Commandant of the Detachment approached the Fentham Trust, requesting permission to use the new village hall as a hospital. Not only did the Trust agree to the request but they offered to defray all costs of heating and lighting from their own funds.

The Men's Institute which had been formed the previous year, based in the original house, also offered to hand over their premises, if required, as an extension to the hospital. In December 1914, the hall became a Red Cross Voluntary Aid Detachment hospital, and the first ten patients were admitted. Two months later, the Fentham Institute handed over their premises and the gardens. In the summer of 1915, a further enlargement was made. A Tee-shaped annex was built from the rear of the Hall, housing a new ward and operating theatre, all funded by private subscriptions from the residents of Knowle and Hampton. Ten more beds were installed, five of which were placed in two small tents on the back lawn. By January 1917 an appeal was made for the supply of more beds. The War Office supplied three Hospital-Marquees, new kitchens and bathrooms were added, fifty more beds were installed and within two weeks they were all filled.

The hospital staff, under the control of a Senior Medical Officer and two Commandants, both matrons, consisted of 22 nursing members, 15 General Administration personnel, 16 orderlies and a large number of local residents who had offered their part-time services. A hostel for the nursing staff was required, and a Mr Simmons offered the use of his furnished property in

The Fentham Club and Hall used as a Red Cross Hospital in the First World War.

Bellemere Road. Later in the war this hostel was moved to one of the Edwardian houses in Meriden Road.

Means of transport for staff and patients was important, and in the first year of the war before the introduction of petrol rationing, this was supplied by the generosity of village residents using their own cars. In September 1917, a village garden fete was held, which provided sufficient funds for the purchase of a small motor ambulance.

Sporting activities continued with reports, in 1915, of bowling on the lawn, by both members of the village and the hospital patients, possibly as a form of physical therapy. At the end of the war Hampton residents received grateful thanks from the War Office and many letters from the military personnel treated at the hospital.

By 1919, the last few patients had left and returned to their homes, and the building was returned to the ownership of the Trust. With the slow return to normal life, the men of the village re-established their men's club, now called the Fentham Institute, and the essential club activities of darts, card games, dominoes, snooker, the occasional drop of alcoholic beverage, and a very active bowling section reappeared. During these inter-war years the club was a very popular haven for the men of the village.

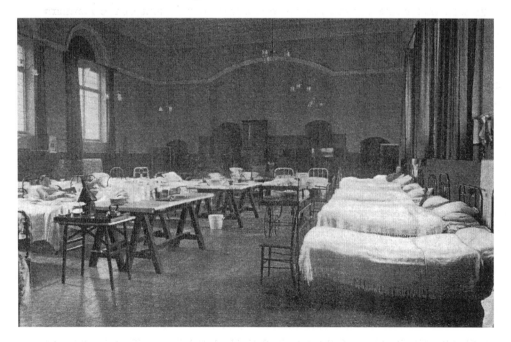

The large hospital ward in 1914 - 1919, now the main Hall.

In the early years of the Second World War the village was host to a large number of evacuees from the cities. Many of these were housed with local residents, a large number in the old vicarage and the remainder in the Fentham Hall, which was used as a dormitory. Then, in early 1943, this quiet little Warwickshire village was to be introduced to a new alien society, which was to affect the lives of this rural community for the next two years. The Americans had arrived!

The headquarters of a Mobile Army Surgical Hospital Unit was set up in the Fentham Hall but unlike the First World War there are no records of it being used as a working hospital. The staff were housed in tents on the lawns or billeted in local homes and a canteen, and the inevitable American services P.X. was built in the old annex. On this occasion, the Club was not affected and continued to serve the needs of the villagers and, no doubt the American servicemen as well. By the end of 1944, the Americans had moved on, and according to comments made by elderly residents who were school children at that time, 'an uncanny silence fell upon the village'.

With the cessation of hostilities the village residents pondered on War Memorials and it was decided that the hall itself should be a memorial as a 'Thanks for Victory'. The various village groups combined and sent out an appeal for funds, in that name, for the improvement and enlargement of the Fentham Hall to be used as a community centre. There was consideration of a stage and dressing rooms with more modern toilet facilities. Between seven and eight hundred pounds were raised, plus an equal amount from covenants, but it was not enough and the idea had to be abandoned. The Trust then came to the rescue and offered a grant equal to the village funds which enabled the building of a new toilet block and kitchen, new ventilators were inserted and a heating boiler was installed. Gradually people came forward with financial and practical help and the refurbishment continued. The walls and roof of the original asbestos annexe were lined with an inner skin and the heating improved. The Women's Institute then decided that they should move from their old headquarters in the Girls School and re-house themselves in the Fentham Annexe. They set to work and carried out further improvements to the appearance of the interior by making and installing curtains.

In the mid 1980s the Trust, enabled by a new trust deed, provided funds for the removal of the old annexe after 70 years of use and to replace it with a small brick building linked to the main hall by a new entrance and toilet block to be known as the Arden Room. This, with the new enlarged kitchen facilities, provided the various village groups with a very high level of comfort, another 'brownie point' for the George Fentham Trust. With this enlarged situation the steward of the Fentham Institute was not able to find time to care for the entire complex and so a new separate caretaker, steward was engaged to oversee the care of the hall.

By now the Fentham Institute had been greatly strengthened as the British Legion had adopted it for their headquarters. The Institute served the men of the village well for many years. Alcoholic refreshments were available, but this was not the primary objective of the establishment. Cards, Dominoes and later snooker were popular games and in the summer the bowling green provided the fresh air and exercise. The Fentham Institute had ceased to provide the more educational facilities of the old Men's Club, it was now purely a social club. It was then decided that lady members should be admitted and so the name Institute was dropped in favour of the Fentham Club. At this time the Club and the Hall were more closely connected. There was a basement common to both buildings, which housed heating boilers fired by coal or coke. The administration and the activities were then carried out by one person, who served as Steward to the Club and Caretaker to the Hall.

A new High Court judgement ruled that such clubs could no longer be considered for charitable funding, and so the relationship between the Fentham Trust and the Fentham Club became strictly Landlord and Tenant. Negotiations with the trust allowed the Institute to pay a rent of £4 per year and the trust paid for all building maintenance. Fortunately the Trust had just completed the work of providing a new attractive lounge overlooking the bowling green and were able to hand it over to the Club as a parting present.

By the late 1980s the British Legion had moved to their new headquarters in Knowle and gradually the membership of the Fentham Club diminished, which brought about the it's closure in November 2003. In 2004 a new leaseholder appeared on the scene and the club was completely refurbished.

Under the new name of The Fentham Grange it became a restaurant and bar, and then one year later, under new management, the bar was removed and the old club became an upmarket restaurant named after the original house – The Beeches.

THE WOMEN'S INSTITUTE

The Women's Institutes across the country constitute several layers; none more important than the other, but all interdependent and interactive. There are local institutes, groups, county, or 'island' federations and the National Federation of Women's Institutes. The N.F.W.I. is made up of W.I. members who give their time to carry out mandates determined by members. It lobbies government and local authorities, and sometimes businesses on matters, which are relevant to uphold the W.I.'s motto 'For Home & Country'. The W.I.'s tenets are fellowship, truth, tolerance and justice. The main purpose of the organisation is to improve the quality of life by enabling women to advance their education in citizenship, the arts and in other cultural subjects, and in branches of agriculture, handicrafts, home economics, health and social welfare.

A newspaper cutting dated 8th May 1940 told us that twenty-one years earlier, in 1919, a Mrs G. Wynne, who lived at a house called 'Rosemary' in Hampton-in-Arden, gathered a few friends who were interested in the movement and founded the Hampton Women's Institute. Members were required to pay a subscription of two shillings. At the time of the coming of age celebrations the one hundred and one members were evidently enjoying themselves, and considered that they were getting value for money. By 1948, they were being asked to find three shillings and six pence each year and the numbers were growing.

In the early years of the life of the Hampton Women's Institute, in addition to the standard format of meetings, garden meetings and fetes were being arranged in the summer months, and whist drives and magic lantern shows in the winter evenings. Programmes were printed informing members, well in advance, of forthcoming events and posters were placed around the village in the attempt to attract and encourage new members. In 1929, it was decided to introduce sub-committees, each responsible for activities which included folk dancing, drama, a variety of handicrafts and the reporting of the monthly events on the club notice board and in the press. The monthly sales table began life in 1933 in the form of a mart. Members would take items for sale, often hand made, or from their gardens. Members were bottling fruit and vegetables for the Midland Hospital and they were organising a produce stall at the village gymkhana in aid of the Village Hall Fund. In this year 40 new members joined, bringing the total to 137. In 1939 the Hampton ladies took part in the Warwick Historical Pageant at Warwick Castle, a grand affair in which they featured in the section depicting The Norman Conquest. A 'Sunshine League' was instituted in this year. Members took on the responsibility of visiting sick or absent members in their area of the village to offer help and comfort.

During the war years, the refreshment secretary successfully battled against the odds. In a time of austerity and rationing, there were no cakes or buns with the traditional cup of tea, and she still managed to make a profit. In 1942, the 'Pie Scheme' began which involved weekly supplies of meat pies to the village. This meant that the Institute had to become registered as a Catering Establishment, working with the Meriden Rural District Food Control Committee. A total of 168 pies were produced each week, and in 1946 nearly 9,000 pies were sold by the Hampton Institute. In 1944, in accordance with the Women's Institute's commitment to public affairs, it was decided that one or two members should attend Parish Council meetings and report proceedings to the committee. There is no record of how long this practice continued or when it ceased.

By 1946 the Institute boasted many specialist sections. Produce Guild members visited and participated in shows in neighbouring towns, distributing seeds, cuttings and plants to be grown by members, and the resulting crops harvested in the following years to enter the chain of need and benefit. Members took on the responsibilities of organising Outings, Food, Refreshments, National Savings and the distribution of the Women's Institutes own magazine, 'Home & Country'. The singers gave concerts and took part in the Combined Arts Festival in Birmingham, the Leamington Musical Festival and also sang at the Royal Albert Hall.

The Infant Welfare Scheme served the mothers of Hampton, distributing orange juice and cod liver oil. Teas were arranged and, with a doctor officiating, the ladies helped with immunisations for diphtheria. Parties and games were organised for the children there was an excellent response for volunteer 'Aunties' to help with children in orphanages. A report in 1927 details an outing to Weston super Mare, by train to Bristol and then a char-a-banc to Weston, costing 19s 10d, including lunch and a meat tea.

During social time at meetings the members participated in a variety of competitions: the best miniature garden, the best pair of knitted socks, best worked buttonhole and the largest grocery parcel for 6d. One winner arranged and named a selection of 32 grasses, and another crammed 132 items into a matchbox to win a prize.

A considerable number of debates were held, on a wide variety of subjects, with very strict rules, members being 'gonged' for irrelevance. In the early days the programme consisted of 'Lectures'; today there are speakers on subjects as varied as, 'Warwickshire Superstitions' and 'Ants and their Habits'. Demonstrations covered cooking, icing cakes and how to make a thrift rug.

The Women's Institute generally relied on the usual fund-raisers, such as jumble sales, marts, whist drives and other entertainments to swell its funds. Subscriptions were never designed to cover all the costs that would be encountered. Members were expected to learn and grow together by co-operation, creativity and effort to raise money to make ends meet. Today, much of the social time often takes place outside the institute, with the enjoyment of garden parties, strawberry teas and luncheons as well as outings and dances.

Recorded lists of organised events at the Hampton Institute meetings show quite clearly that life was never boring and gives a clear indication that the lady members were not only very innovative in all their activities, but also showed an extremely caring attitude to others in need.

SCOUTS & GUIDES

Much of the early history of the Hampton Scouts and Guides appears as reports and articles in the Church Chronicle, the first in the February issue of 1922.

In January a meeting was held in the Church Hall to assist Mr R. G. Hollick, named as the Scoutmaster, to form a Hampton scout group, which would be affiliated to the Knowle Association. This group would be self-supporting, with members paying for their uniform and equipment by weekly subscriptions. To provide initial funding a concert was to be held in the Fentham Hall. There was obviously no delay in the organisation of this event because in the March issue of the chronicle there appears a detailed report of this concert, attended by Major Everitt, the District Commissioner, parents and friends and the scout groups from Knowle and Yardley. The items of entertainment were typical of the day, with a variety of songs, banjo and violin solos and musical sketches. Mr James Rollason, of Hampton Manor, consented to become the first President of the local Scouts Committee and it was reported that – 'Several Gentlemen of the village have agreed to serve'.

An early photograph of Hampton Guides, date unknown.

In the same month it was reported that both the Girl Guides and Boy Scouts were to be heartily congratulated on their recent debut in the parish. The Guides and Brownies paraded at the Ring of Bells Assembly Room, with their captain Miss Goodwin and lieutenant, Miss Jevons, and after taking the oath of loyalty to God and the King they were presented with their enrolment badges.

In August 1925 the scouts attended a summer camp in Holt, Worcestershire. The subsequent report in the chronicle stated that the 'Wolves' rowed six miles up the river, and at some point the 'Lions' rowed back. A visit was made to Worcester Royal Porcelain, followed by an excellent lunch donated by the Vicar, and then to other places of interest. With the inevitable songs round the campfire, games, sports and other scout practices it was a successful trip.

In May 1931 the Guides held a concert in Fentham Hall consisting of a mixture of Country Dances and Plays. Mrs Eddington, the Captain, was thanked for paying £2 2s for the hire of the Hall.

In September of this year the Scout group, or presumably the adult association behind them, held their first Whist Drive at the Church House, organised by Mr Wilfred Martin, the new scoutmaster. The prizes consisted of a tea tray, an umbrella and a brush rack, all of which were donated by local residents.

In August 1935 the report stated – 'the exploring band of Hampton Rover Scouts will now be camping on their 'desert-island' off the coast of Sweden. They formed a small part of 5,000 Rovers and Scouts from many countries. At the same time the Guides had to be satisfied with a camping holiday in Dawlish.

Jean Bulpitt ran the Guide Company for several years before the Second World War, followed by Kay Newey until 1949 when Pam Greenway took over. Pam was always keen on camping and outdoor activities and has fond memories of the Guides always being welcome on land belonging to the Bulpitt family, and especially in an area of woodland that they owned in Marston Green. A dedicated Parents Association raised a considerable amount of money to provide for all the necessary camping equipment. The girls travelled to camp every summer and also had weekend camps on the field next to the old wooded scout hut. The Guides had regular parades, marching one month to the Parish Church and the next to the Chapel in Butchers Road. In 1949 they won the Division Shield for their marching and on a number of other occasions for smart camps, cooking and first aid activities. The Company also went on several residential outdoor activity weeks in Wales and Gloucestershire in addition to the annual camps. Twice, in 1980 and 1987, the older girls had the opportunity to travel to the Guide Chalet in Switzerland where, on each occasion, they spent two wonderful weeks in the company of Guides from other countries.

Unfortunately, log books relating to Scout and Guide activities after the Second World War have been mislaid, so very little information remains other than the memories of past leaders.

For a short time in the 1960s the Scout Troop ceased to exist, but then was re-opened by John Robinson, the Scoutmaster in 1965. For a number of years he held annual campfire evenings at the Old Girls School in an attempt to attract new members. The 850-Year Church Scrapbook records a special church parade and service in September 1965, when the old scout flag was replaced by a new Colour, which was dedicated, blessed and paraded at the service. When John Robinson finally retired, in about 1998, no successor could be found and the Troop was disbanded.

In 1971 the old wooden scout hut was moved to its present location to make way for the new squash courts at the Sports Club. At first the hut was attached to a brick frontage and then was finally replaced with a new brick building, thanks to the fund raising of the Supporters Committee and the generous donations made by local residents, businesses and the Fentham Trust. This new Scout and Guide headquarters was officially opened by the Chief Scout, Mr W. Garth Morrison, on May 15th 1994.

Guides, Cubs, Brownies and Rainbows are still active. The Brownie Pack, which was first registered in 1922, has always been popular. For some time prior to 1940 the Pack was run by Alice Cox followed by Joan Lyons (nee Hunt) during the war and then once again in the 1950s. A second Pack was established in 1980, as there were so many wishing to join. Both Packs had new colours dedicated and blessed at a church parade later that year. In 1999 the two were joined into one group through the loss of a guider and the difficulty of finding a replacement. Unfortunately there appears to be an increasing lack of interest by older children in joining this form of group activity, and not only in Hampton. Comments from past Guiders seem to show that the problem is more a lack of adult interest and the willingness to become involved. For the sake of those children who want to belong, we can only hope that this downturn can be overcome in the future.

CHAPTER THIRTEEN

Famous Residents

We have mentioned two residents in this book, George Fentham and Sir Frederick Peel, both of whom left their mark on the village. We must also include some residents who did not necessarily leave their mark on the village but are worthy of comment.

Two railwaymen of note lived in the village and lived virtually under the same roof, they were James (later Sir James) Allport and Matthew Kirtley. The two men and their families shared Vale House, the property of the Birmingham and Derby Junction Railway, which connected Hampton (and the main Birmingham to London line) with Derby. Matthew Kirtley was the Locomotive Superintendent and James Allport was the Station Clerk effectively Station Master.

James Allport was born in Birmingham in 1811 the son of a gunmaker. He considered that the railways were the thing of the future and in 1839 he applied and obtained a job with the new railway line aimed at linking Derby with a fast line to London. He rapidly became a force to be reckoned with and in 1842 he was promoted to be Traffic Manager based in Birmingham. The merging of three railway companies in 1844 left him without a job but his worth was recognised and, in 1853, after a number of posts he became General Manager of the Midland Railway. He was a pioneer of better conditions for the poorer travellers and also introduced Pullman Car travel. He was responsible for the opening of the Settle and Carlisle line, was knighted in 1884 and died in 1892.

Matthew Kirtley came from a railway family and on the opening of the London to Birmingham line in 1838 he was reputed to have driven the first train from Euston to Birmingham (Curzon Street). On the formation of the Birmingham and Derby Junction railway he became foreman at Hampton in charge of the four engines based in Hampton. In 1844 on the merger of three railway companies Matthew Kirtley became Locomotive Superintendent for the resulting Midland Railway Company. He was to be in charge of the Derby base until his death in 1873. He was responsible for a number of innovations in locomotive design.

Humphrey Francis Humphries was a well-known resident, he lived in Church House in Solihull Road, during and after the second World War and was the first president of the Hampton Society. He was born in Bromsgrove on June 19th, 1855 and moved to Edgbaston in 1893 where his father had a dental practice. Educated at Bromsgrove School he entered the medical and dental courses at Birmingham University simultaneously in 1903. After graduating he spent 6 months as a postgraduate student at the dental school of Harvard University and then spent six months travelling the world. He then joined his father's dental practice. In 1914 he volunteered for active service, joining the Second South Midland Mounted Brigade Field Ambulance and served with it for nearly five years spending most of the time in the Middle East. His bravery in action, in which he evacuated badly wounded men on his own back, earned him the first of three Mentions in Despatches, while for his part in Allenby's Jerusalem Campaign he was awarded the M.C.

In 1922 he helped raise an Infantry Field Ambulance in the Territorial Army which he commanded until 1930 when he was appointed Assistant Director of Medical Services of the 48th (South Midland) Division. His contributions to the Territorial Army were recognised by the award of an O.B.E. in 1928 and appointment as King's Honorary Physician in 1934. He was appointed a Deputy Lieutenant of Warwickshire in 1935 and in the same year was appointed the first full-time Professor of Dental Surgery in the University of Birmingham.

After the Munich Crisis in 1938 he was invited to raise a field hospital in Birmingham which became the 14th General Hospital. After the outbreak of war, the hospital spent periods in Europe and then embarked for India and later Burma. After the war he returned to Birmingham University becoming Vice-Principal in 1949. He retired in 1953 but spent an active life on various national and international committees. He was appointed a Commander of the Order of the British Empire in 1957. He died in 1977.

James Valentine Jelley was a well-known artist who lived in Caxton House in Bellemere Road from about 1896 to 1920. He was born in Lincoln in 1856 but moved to Birmingham and was on the staff of the Birmingham School of Art for 40 years. He exhibited regularly in Birmingham between 1878 and 1942 - some 203 paintings in all. He also exhibited at the Royal Academy showing 23 works between 1884 and 1891. His range of subjects was wide: everything except portraits. Rural and coastal scenes, flowers and genre subjects attracted him more than others. He was elected an associate of the Royal Birmingham Society of Artists in 1884 and a member in 1891. He died in 1950 and is buried in Hampton Churchyard.

Ernest Albert Chadwick was born on 29th February 1876 at Marston Green. The son of a draughtsman and wood engraver. He showed an early aptitude for drawing and painting and later studied art in Birmingham. He lived at Canterbury House at the top of Marsh Lane.

During the Second World War the man responsible for testing all of the spitfires built at Castle Bromwich, Alex Henshaw, lived in Old Station Road, or Birmingham Road as it then was. He flew his own plane to and from work landing it in a field behind his house making sure the anti-aircraft gunners were aware of his flights. This is detailed in his book "Sigh for a Merlin" which describes his activities as Chief Test Pilot for the Spitfires produced at Castle Bromwich. But Alex had a distinguished career up until the war as an aviation pioneer. In February 9th 1939, he flew from England to Capetown and back in a Percival Mew Gull in 4 days 10 hours 20 minutes setting a new record.

CHAPTER FOURTEEN

Happenings in Hampton

From the late 1800s to the mid 1930s a weekly newspaper was printed called the Birmingham News. On one page of this newspaper, each week there appeared a collection of articles headed, News and Views from Villages around Birmingham. Over these years a succession of people in Hampton took the trouble to collect and compile some interesting happenings in the village.

April 28th 1900. Hampton-in-Arden Parish Council gave permission to change the name Back Lane to Fentham Road.

July 12th 1902. A proposal put to the Parish Council by Mr Tall, publican of the Ring of Bells for the provision of a village Recreation Ground, and on September 13th the council met to discuss the purchase of a piece of ground. The decision was postponed. (It was to be a further sixty three years, in 1965, before a village Recreation Ground was formed).

December 12th 1908. The Men's Recreational Club, Air Gun Club competition. This was active until 1914, re-commenced in 1919 but eventually folded through lack of funds and a suitable venue.

January 16th 1909. The first recorded 'Weather Report' from the Manor rain gauge. Hottest Day (138 deg. F in full sun) - June 4th 1908. Coldest Day (24 deg. of frost) - December 30th 1908.

February 13th 1909. A burglary was foiled in the early hours of the morning at Mr Burrill's shop opposite the Church. Burglars attempted to remove a 32lb ham hanging in the window. The window was broken with a brick wrapped in a blanket. The ham could not be pulled through the small glass panes and fell into the shop breaking several jars of jam. The noise woke residents asleep in rooms above the shop. The police reported that the burglars fled without their 'booty'.

May 21st 1910. An aeroplane in the experimental stage, being the design and property of Messrs Morton and Wheeler, a Coventry firm, manufactured from Aluminium and Bamboo with a wing span of 48 feet was flown this week from a field in Hampton. The plane was attached in sections to the sides and roof of two cars at the company's premises in Cox Street, Coventry and driven, then assembled in Hampton. The result was a successful flight of about a quarter of a mile.

January 28th 1911. The first discussions of starting a Hampton Scout Group. Mr G. Chavasse (Pres). Mr W. Nash.(Sec. & Treas.) Mr. R. Hughes (Sc. Leader) G. Glover & W. Fodin (Sc. Ass'ts).

October 7th 1911. There were complaints at a Council Meeting of continual blockage by horses and carts in Fentham Road on Sale Day, and the bad language of the drovers.

December 11th 1911. At a Parish Council meeting it was proposed that the 'Glebe Land' on Fentham Road should be sold to the trustees of the Fentham Charity for the site of a new Boys School.

March 16th 1912. Coal Strike – adverse effect on the railway, trains up to one hour late.

November 9th 1912. There was a large gathering of ladies at 'Glenthorn', the house of Mrs Nash, for a suffragette meeting.

February 1913. The Ladies Parish Tea was held at the Ring of Bells Inn. The Vicar made a comment, which was more of a rumour, that the George Fentham Trust would be providing a Village Club House in the near future.

September 27th 1913. A decision was made by the George Fentham Trustees to light the Fentham Institute by means of an electric installation. The local Red Cross detachment has just received official recognition by the War Office as a fully qualified unit of the National Voluntary Aid Detachment, to be known as Detachment 50.

February 1914. Travelling Dairy School. A course of instruction in dairy work, butter and cheese making, by Miss Ingliss N.D.D., county instructress, to be held at the Ring of Bells Inn.

May 9th 1914. Hampton-in-Arden Boys School is to be opened on May 20th by councillor Innis Bates B.Sc. of the Coventry Education Committee.

February 1918. German prisoners of war brought to Mercote Hall for farm labouring.

May 1918. Hampton Bowling Green re-opened after extensions carried out. Now voted the best green in the Midlands.

June 1918. Sister Wilson, the joint commandant of Hampton Red Cross hospital has been presented with the Royal Red Cross Medal by King George at Buckingham Palace.

July 1918. The Red Cross hospital at Fentham Hall has been closed temporarily due to the reduced numbers of patients.

September 1918. Red Cross hospital re-opened with a new intake of patients. Proposed sale of the pound by the Lady Peel. (This animal enclosure was sited in Fentham Road, where the garage to number 72 is now).

January 1919. Lady Peel gave a piece of land to the north of the church as an extension of the churchyard. (Now the car park and site of the Church Hall).

March 21st 1919. The Red Cross hospital used for military personnel during the war, based in Fentham Institute, was finally closed today.

April 1919. The Red Cross hospital offered the return of the premises to the village for a small cost in their appreciation of the help given by the residents throughout the war. Built by them as extra ward space, valued at £450. A Red Cross sale of surplus effects brought a total of £720. The Ford Motor Ambulance, purchased from the proceeds of a village fete, fetched £190.

May 1919. A dance has been planned at the newly restored Fentham Hall. The first discussions were made, at 'Rosemary' the residence of Mrs G. Wynne, of opening a Women's Institute in Hampton.

June 1919. The Fentham Institute opened its doors to members on Saturday, May 31st, in the premises previously used as the Red Cross hospital. The house provided by Mr Jacques as a church room during the war has been restored as a private residence. The room in the Boys School, recently vacated by the Men's Club who have now moved to the Fentham Institute is to be used as a church meeting room.

October 1919. The Parish Council met to discuss the design and site of a War Memorial. Mr Rollason, owner of the Manor is to be asked about the availability of the triangle of ground opposite the railway station.

April 1921. War trophies, a German Field Gun on a solid foundation placed in front of the Fentham Institute. Rifles displayed on racks inside. Hampton homes were without coal for heating during a coal strike.

May 1921. Coal has been supplied to some village homes from stocks at the Boys School. Hampton Nursing Association has hopes of building a Cottage Hospital in the village. They are looking in the area of the old Red Cross hospital at Fentham Hall.

July 9th 1921. The building of Hampton-in-Arden War Memorial commenced this week. The foundation and base has been laid. The memorial cross is to be unveiled by the Bishop of Birmingham on July 23rd.

August 1921. There have been many 'town' visitors to the village. This has caused problems and concern over groups of 'rowdy youths' setting up tents and looting the fruit trees in the gardens.

September 1921. A ploughing match was held by the Hampton Farmers Union.

November 1921. A Hampton Fire Brigade has been established. Harvey Burrill to be the senior officer. Discussion of fire hydrants placed around the village as only 16 houses could be tackled if a fire started. Suggested positions – High Street, opposite the Girls School; Fentham Road, opposite Mr Peploes house, Elm Lodge; Birmingham Road, Mr Cox's Station Farm and Café; and The Crescent near Glenthorne.

January 1922. Decision by 173 members of the Fentham Institute to double the subscription.

June 3rd 1922. The Bishop of Birmingham consecrated the new piece of ground, to the north of the church, given by Lady Peel, as an extension of the churchyard.

June 8th 1922. The first bus service from Solihull to Hampton. Fare 6d each way.

June 10th 1922. Whit Monday – Over 1,300 visitors, on specially arranged excursions by rail and road, came to visit the 'Beautiful Village of Hampton-in-Arden' The villagers opened their gardens and provided visitors with tea and refreshments. It was said to be hard work but financially rewarding.

July 1922. The Women's Institute moved to the Old Boys' Schoolroom. There was an outing to Hampton from one of the poorest areas of Birmingham. 80 members of the Mothers Union were brought on 3 'Four Horse' Drawn Charabancs. A walk through the village, a visit to the church, games in the vicarage garden and tea at The Spinney, by Mr & Mrs Jacques.

1923. The formation of an 'Arden Club' with a monthly meeting at The Engine. This is a mixed club with lunch and entertainments.

December 1st 1923. Hampton-in-Arden Service Men's Club officially joined the British Legion. It is to be based in the Fentham Institute. President – Colonel Nutt. Officers – Colonel Bourne, Major Phillips, Lt. Henderson, Lt. Jevons. Committee – H. Burrill, P. King, R. Townley, W. Hill, A. Austin.

March 1924. A British Legion Dance was held in the Fentham Hall. The George Fentham Trust accounts. From Rents and Properties, a total of £2,223 9s 7d. Expenditure on estates – £109, Charitable purchases – £118, Pay to Educational Foundation – £500, Costs – Fentham Hall £532, Miscellaneous – £141.

April 1924. Alexander William Hemming, of The Elms was fined 40s, for allowing 4 cattle to stray, and breaking a Foot and Mouth Disease Order.

June 1924. Harvey Burrill retires as Head of the Fire Brigade after 3 years. There have been complaints of the dangerous driving of cars and motorbikes through the village, especially at weekends.

August 1924. Boy Scouts group cycled to Snowdon and back on a Welsh cycling tour. A fire on the stairs of Hampton Railway Station was dealt with by the Fire Brigade. Miss King has retired as Postmistress after 48 years.

November 15th 1924. The first collection of letters from a post box in the wall of the L.M.S. station occurred today. Mr H. Burrill was granted a licence by the Birmingham Postmaster General to sell postage stamps from the village shop.

February 21st 1925. The presentation of an Eight Day Clock was made today to Mr Felix Borley, a member of the Hampton-in-Arden Fire Brigade, by the retired Chief Fire Officer, Mr Harvey Burrill. (The report did not specify the reason for the presentation).

January 1930. Planning has begun to widen the Railway Bridge at Hampton Station.

HAMPTON-IN-ARDEN SOCIETY

Established to maintain the character of the village and its environments. The Society was formed in 1966 with the following objectives: To stimulate public interest in the Civic Parish of Hampton-in-Arden and its surroundings. To promote high standards of planning and architecture in the Civic Parish of Hampton-in-Arden and it surroundings. To secure the preservation and protection, development and improvement of features of historic or public interest in the Civic Parish of Hampton-in-Arden and its surroundings.

INDEX